GOOD NEIGHBOURHOOD
AND OTHER ADDRESSES
IN THE UNITED STATES

GOOD NEIGHBOURHOOD

AND OTHER ADDRESSES
IN THE UNITED STATES

BY THE HON.
VINCENT MASSEY, P.C. (*Can.*), LL.D.

". . . and thereby to promote
a disposition favourable to
friendship and good neighbourhood . . . "

*Treaty of Amity, Commerce and
Navigation (Jay's Treaty), 1794.*

Essay Index Reprint Series

BOOKS FOR LIBRARIES PRESS
FREEPORT, NEW YORK

First Published 1930
Reprinted 1969

LIBRARY OF CONGRESS CATALOG CARD NUMBER:

69-17584

PRINTED IN THE UNITED STATES OF AMERICA

TO MY WIFE

PREFACE

If it be true that the making of speeches is a practice to be condoned only with difficulty, then the publication of such utterances after their delivery is even harder to defend. Some justification for such a course may perhaps be found in the fact that the printing of the spoken word offers the public a comforting immunity from hearing the same observations repeated on succeeding occasions. But a more serious reason may be offered as an apology for yielding to the suggestions of friends that such fugitive speeches as these should be committed to print. "Extenuating circumstances" in this case may be discovered in the subjects themselves. Some of these are related to Canada's new departure in diplomacy, while others have real importance, too, however slight the significance of what is said in this volume about them. If random addresses can serve in some small way to encourage further thinking about the problems with which they venture to deal, there may be some grounds for giving them a slightly longer life than would have been theirs in spoken form alone.

To the indulgent audiences who heard these various speeches the speaker will be always grateful; of the reader he could ask no greater forbearance.

V. M.

Batterwood House,
 Port Hope,
  27th September, 1930.

CONTENTS

xi

CONTENTS

CANADA'S FIRST LEGATION

*Before the Pilgrims of the
United States at a Dinner of
Welcome, New York, 23rd
February, 1927*

Mr. Chairman and Gentlemen:

May I thank you with all my heart for the
generous welcome you have given me to-night.
It is but another evidence of the cordiality and
sincerity with which Canada's first Minister
to the United States has been met everywhere
since his arrival in your midst, and which represents a most graceful compliment to my
country.

When I had the honour of presenting my
Letter of Credence to your President, I was
conscious that the envoy from Canada was
received by the head of your great Republic
in a spirit of real friendship. And the courtesy and sincerity of the official welcome which
I received at the hands of your chief executive has gracefully symbolized the reception
which everywhere has been given to our new
mission.

May I say that the legation which your

government is shortly to establish in Canada we regard as a further demonstration of this attitude of goodwill? You have honoured Canada by the appointment of a distinguished gentleman to serve as your first minister at Ottawa. It will not be inappropriate for me to say that Mr. Phillips's advent is looked forward to with great interest and with sincere pleasure by all of us, and especially by those who have the privilege of knowing him personally and are familiar with his qualities. A very cordial and a very genuine welcome awaits him in Ottawa and throughout the entire Dominion.

I am not altogether sure that I have shown the part of discretion in accepting this charming invitation to address you, and I will tell you why. I have recently been engaged in a self-prescribed course of study for new and unfamiliar duties (you will agree that this is the part of wisdom) and the other day, when I was quite appropriately turning the pages of a work on diplomatic practice, I came across a letter written by Lord Malmesbury, the celebrated Georgian diplomatist, for the purpose of giving counsel to a friend's son who was about to enter the diplomatic service. The most significant passage read as follows: "The first and best advice I can give a young man

on entering this career is *to listen, not to talk*".
However, gentlemen, although I have rashly
been led to depart from such wise counsel, I
am most happy to have the opportunity of
making my first speech as Canadian Minister
to the United States before this distinguished
society. I know something of the great traditions of the Pilgrims. I am familiar with your
ideals and the noble contributions which the
society has made to the cause of strengthening
the friendship which exists and must ever
exist between the peoples of the United States
and the British Empire.

To think of the fine role of interpreter which
you have played so well through the years
gives peculiar pleasure to a Canadian guest.
It has become almost a truism to say that Canada herself is destined to play the part of an
interpreter between her great neighbour and
her Mother Country overseas. Canadians are
on the same high pilgrimage of international
amity and goodwill as is your society. After
all we feel we know you who live just across
our border and can understand in some measure and can appreciate the intricate and fascinating pattern which modern American life
presents. On the other hand we have too a
first-hand knowledge of, and an abiding affection for, the great mother nation whose im-

press has been placed upon our institutions and our national life. This role of interpreter may sound rhetorical and remote from fact; let me make it concrete. I believe it is a part which individual Canadians love to play. Look in the smoking-room of an Atlantic liner and if you find there a citizen from my country you are as likely as not to hear him either telling an Englishman what good fellows the Americans are when one gets to know them, or assuring an American that the Englishman is a first-rate chap.

Gentlemen, in all the great world of international affairs there is no nobler cause to serve than that of deepening the understanding between your great Republic and the nations of what we still call—although the term has long been an anachronism—the British Empire. There is no occasion before such an audience as this to lay stress on those fundamental things which our people enjoy in common. The two civilizations have sprung from a common root; the great, deep-laid, unshakeable foundations are the same. We all of us believe—and this conception is not so generally accepted in the world at large as once it was—that people should be allowed, even asked, to govern themselves, and that they should bear in common the consequences of their own self-government—which is in itself self-education. The American nation and the British peoples are united in an unconquerable love of peace, a determination to "seek peace and ensue it" wherever their fortunes lead. Human affairs in both are guided by a vivid moral sense—the legacy of the Puritanism which seventeenth century England bequeathed to the English-speaking world. We have inherited the same common law whose genius, as one of your own great jurists has put it, is "experience, not logic". In other words the law under which we all live is not the child of theory but is founded upon practical realities. We are heirs to a common literature. It is perhaps true that those of us who speak the English tongue—and let us not forget that there are many among what we call the English-speaking peoples who do not—even those whose language is English, can hardly, as is sometimes affirmed in confident tones, be said to "speak the tongue that Shakespeare spake". But there is a language greater than a spoken tongue, and it is in this spiritual language, the language of common ideals—that the American and British peoples can speak to each other. And whenever some great convulsion shakes the world the Atlantic is spanned by this common tongue, for I believe that there could be no crisis such as has threatened

society of late and one day may do so again—
in which the United States and the British
peoples would not be found standing shoulder
to shoulder.

Now, I quite realize that I may be incurring
the displeasure of the cynic who utters that
terrible, accusing word "sentimentality" and
says something scornful about old fashioned
clichés like "hands across the sea" and "blood
is thicker than water". Well, we all hate
clichés, tags of speech when they are used
simply as tags. (It is ironical that one is so
often conscious even at dinner of Stevenson's
epigram that "man lives not by bread alone
but principally upon catchwords".) We may
agree with our critic in this and we can follow
him also when he points out the differences—
growing differences—which more and more
mark the new country as departing from the
traditions of the old in literature, the arts,
education, business life, public administration,
law itself. It is true—this divergence—this
growing dissimilarity. But what could be
more healthy? It is in fact regrettable that in
North America your country and mine have
in many respects been slow and even reluctant
to develop each for itself its own peculiar
forms of expression true to its origin and environment.

I believe that Anglo-American friendship rests on the frank recognition of existing differences in outlook and in method, rather than on any well-meant exaggeration of similarity. As a matter of fact the readiness to respect and safeguard the customs and characteristics, even the prejudices, of a community is in itself a fundamental attribute of the Anglo-Saxon wherever he lives. The British Empire endures because of the respect for national self-expression which is enshrined in its system. Among the Dominions represented around the Imperial Conference table last autumn in London were three in which the languages of minorities are given official sanction and protection. In your own country the great principle of federalism was first tried on a vast scale and exists as the solution of the very problem of reconciling local rights with national unity. Its success needs no comment from me.

National characteristics are not an obstacle to international amity. They give colour to life in a world where standardization has become a peril. I find little attractiveness in that anaemic cosmopolitanism that offers a pallid ideal to some theorists. A nationalism controlled and directed towards peaceful rivalries should be a force for good. Mazzini said, "A nation is the workshop of the world"; therefore let us welcome those divergences of custom and method even among those nations most closely related. By such national distinctions is their existence as nations justified. It is the task of that much-abused profession—diplomacy—to understand and interpret these differences. It is essential to know that while the United States and the British nations rest on the same foundations, the superstructure is built in different architectural styles and the higher the buildings go, metaphorically speaking, the more outwardly unlike will the structures be.

Unity in diversity is a key to Anglo-American relations. It has too a bearing on those international relations on the continent which we who are here to-night know best. After all, harmony in music comes only when different notes are struck together. Harmony among nations comes only when each remains true to its own background, performs its own proper and peculiar task, and respects the other's point of view. There are two lines of that good Victorian, Tennyson, which it seems to me possess deep wisdom in their application to this question:

> . . . God fulfills Himself in many ways,
> Lest one good custom should corrupt the world.

One custom, however good, would be bad for
the world; it would not be in the interests even
of this continent where it is well that there
should be a diversity in nation building.

In Canada we know something of your
achievements. We are familiar with what
you are doing from close at hand and can appreciate the contributions which you have already given to the world: the organization of
industry in this country which is so impressive; the high standard of living throughout
your land which is a source of amazement to
your visitors; the manner in which education
is brought within the grasp of all, irrespective
of all handicaps, economic or physical. Such
passionate faith in education cannot be
surpassed elsewhere. Again, no other community can rival the record of the United States
in the extent to which private wealth is directed to the public good. Your great private
trusts and foundations, whose operations
know no national boundaries, are an inspiration to benefactors the world over. Again,
throughout the country your cities and towns
are blazing new trails in bringing the arts into
direct touch with the people. Music and painting, through such democratization, are becoming a necessity for the many instead of a luxury for the few. And so on—I should like to

give you more of a visitor's, a neighbour's impressions, but time will not permit: and also I am a little conscious of a moral which was conveyed in a story once told in this city by Sir Edwin Arnold. In referring to the greatness of this country he said that the most elaborate panegyric would seem but an impertinence which would only remind his hearers, perhaps too vividly, of Sidney Smith who, when he saw his grandchild pat the back of a large turtle, ask her why she did so. The little girl replied: "Grandfather, I do it to please the turtle." "My child," he answered, "you might just as well stroke the dome of St. Paul's to please the Dean and Chapter."

Well, gentlemen, I have no desire to pat the back of the turtle to-night, although I know that the turtle would be entirely amiable, but perhaps you will let me tell you that those of us who from beyond your border are watching your colossal achievement in civilization can only sincerely admire the spirit of the pioneer which you have so finely preserved: your high-spirited faith in the future, the refusal to look back, the magnificent team-play with which every task is undertaken.

We in Canada, in turn, to be true to our trusteeship have our own work to perform. Like yours it comes of our own peculiar background and our natural orientation. In years gone by one has heard it said that in North America there is no justification for two English-speaking nations, and that one should ultimately be merged with the other. Such a view, however seriously it may once have been held, now smacks only of the distant past. The idea that there should be a fusion between our two democracies now belongs either to the sphere of the antiquarian or the humorist.

The invisible boundary which runs between us is not a frontier, thank heaven, and never will be. A sentry on the international border between your country and mine would be about as appropriate as a fire-extinguisher on the top of the Great Pyramid. The boundary is not a frontier; it is not even a point of separation. I like to think of it rather as merely a line of demarcation where two nations will meet perpetually in friendship and goodwill. The relations between Canada and the United States for upwards of a century have been an example to the world. When problems have arisen between us we have given them prompt and workmanlike settlement. Our relations have constantly been improved until one can speak of them in terms of cordial friendship without the least risk of overstatement, and it is the hope and intention of the government

and people of Canada that their legation in
your capital—and I need not say that this is
shared by its first Minister—that their legation will serve to strengthen and perpetuate
the goodwill which already exists.

On each side of the international line there
is I believe to be found an increased respect
for the traditions and political institutions
that prevail on the other. Commercial relations bring knowledge and understanding.
The growth of trade between our countries,
which can only be to our mutual advantage
and profit, will result in the widening of this
knowledge and understanding and, following
that, in an even greater mutual respect. The
economic intercourse between us has no aim
beyond itself. We know that when you invest
your capital in Canadian securities you have
but one motive—simply to place your money
in what we believe Canada can provide, and is
glad to provide for you, a sound investment.

I can relieve your feelings too, Mr. Chairman, by assuring you that Canada has mag-
nanimously abandoned any ambition she may
have had to take forcible possession of her
southern neighbours. Sometimes when I see
the names of so many Canadians in strategical
positions in your banks, on your hospital
staffs, in your insurance companies, in your

universities, it seems difficult to explain that their presence betrays no sinister intention on our part. However, may I say that this peaceful penetration from the north expresses but a neighbourly desire to help and that at your own kind invitation.

It is an interesting fact that the professions which seem to be most popular with Canadians in the United States are those to which the Scotsman naturally gravitates, for example, that of an actuary—a special preserve of the Scot. I believe that in the actuarial societies of the United States, a substantial proportion is represented by Canadians. Perhaps in a nation that has been called the Scotland of North America it may not be unreasonable to have inherited some of the characteristics of Scotia herself. One of these is Scotland's immemorial habit of acquiring posts of influence across her southern border for her native sons. There is another trait of character which we may have inherited from Scotland. It has been observed that the ancient passion for national self-depreciation which has run in the blood of England for so long encounters an almost total immunity north of the Tweed. We Canadians too have an enthusiasm for our national future which I hope you will admit is forgivable and even appropriate in a young people.

I have no intention to-night of giving you figures to illustrate the economic development of Canada. As a matter of fact I do not believe in statistics after dinner. But it is a source of quiet pride to Canadians to recognize certain facts that mark our progress. For instance, our country is now the greatest exporter of wheat in the world. Year by year the margin of cultivation is pushed further north and the intensification of farming is proceeding, until the great north west of Canada, as it receives the settlers it still needs, will become the greatest source of the world's cereal food stuffs. Again, we are rapidly developing our great mining areas. We have become, for example, the third greatest exporter of gold in the world. Northern Ontario, Quebec and Manitoba conceal beneath their vast pre-Cambrian shield minerals of nearly every kind. The surface has merely been scratched as yet, and this great region harbours under its rock-bound face mineral treasure which will stagger the imagination of the most sanguine prospector. So much for such facts. There is now a rising tide of prosperity in my country which has engulfed the few pessimists who remained. Despite the legacy left by four and a half years of war and the world-wide depression which followed it, we have emerged completely and entirely and have entered upon one of those epochs of swift advancement and assured prosperity which are the natural possessions of a young country with courage and resourcefulness and the possession of vast natural wealth. One knows at all events that there is none of the various indices of economic progress which does not give striking evidence, and in many cases record the highwater mark, of development up to the present. A spirit of optimism is universal, and trade, domestic and international, is flourishing. If this sounds like a burst of boastfulness encouraged by your kind indulgence and the hospitable atmosphere of this room, I ask you to submit my optimism to the stern test of your own observation. Come and see us. I can assure you that whether your visit be one of business or pleasure, or even made out of pardonable curiosity —to see what manner of folk we are—you will be given a welcome from the heart, and I believe you will find that northern hospitality is no less warm and sincere than that hospitality of yours—whose fame is justly so great.

I have spoken of some of the natural gifts with which my country is endowed. We like

to feel that there are other non-material contributions which we have made—intangible
and perhaps sometimes forgotten—which give
added meaning to our national existence. It
has been our lot in the last few generations to
solve some problems in the science of government which had hitherto defeated the statesman. These successful efforts have all been
in the sphere of reconciliation—the harmon-
ization of what had hitherto been opposing
forces. In the first place we have demonstrated that two races each possessing its own
traditions and culture can live in harmony
within the borders of a single state. The
French-Canadian minority in Canada enjoys
the precious rights of language and religion
just as the English-speaking minority in Quebec is given like privileges. As a Canadian
from an English-speaking province I should
like to say, what I know to be true, that the
two and a half million French-speaking Canadian citizens bring to our common country
a strain of culture which lends great richness
to our national life. The ancient civilization
of Quebec with its historic faith, its beautiful
tongue and the charm of its manners and the
romance of its background, gives to Canada a
priceless asset, as those of you who visit that
province know.

Secondly, not only have we reconciled French and English in Canada, but we have done something more difficult. Seventy-five years ago we proved that the assumption of self-government by a colony did not weaken, but rather strengthened, the real bonds which joined it to the Mother Country. It was on Canadian soil that the foundations of the modern British Commonwealth were laid by a combination of Canadian courage and British statecraft. Three-quarters of a century before that time you had proved on this side of the border that the old British Empire with its rigid, inflexible system could not survive. It was for us later on, acting on your experience, to show that with a new-found imagination and elasticity the new British Empire could live and prosper. You and we, if you will let me say so, are therefore collaborators in creating this modern British Commonwealth.

You and we have co-operated in another way, and this leads to the third great task which we in Canada have undertaken. It was the example of your successful achievement which led our statesmen just sixty years ago this year, to employ the federal system, modified, of course, to suit our own circumstances, as the basis of the new Canadian nation which had its birth in 1867. They did a very bold thing: they erected a British parliamentary structure on a federal foundation. It had never been done before. It has been done since in Australia and in South Africa. Canada was the first child of a union between the British system adapted to our needs, with a constitutional monarch—represented with us by a Governor-General who acts in all essentials as the King—on the one hand, and on the other, a federal union of provinces, now nine in number, each again possessing the same British parliamentary system on a smaller scale. The marriage has been a most happy one with no demand for dissolution or provision for it— a pleasant and unusual picture in these modern days.

Lastly, there is another great development, another reconciliation of principles in which Canada has taken her full share. I refer to those steps in the last nine years in which the British Empire took its present, and as I believe its permanent form, in which the freedom of the part was perfectly reconciled with the unity of the whole. The Empire is now a free association of nations under a single Sovereign. It might be possible to apply to this Commonwealth an old formula in a new sense and say that its members are joined together in "Liberty, Equality and Fraternity" under their common Crown. And it may truly be said that the sense of "Fraternity" amongst them has been strengthened by the recognition of their "Liberty" and "Equality".

The new diplomatic enterprise of my own Dominion—with which I have the honour to be associated—is one more concrete evidence of the relationships which prevail within the modern British Empire. I should like to say that this new step of ours was taken not only with the fullest approval, but with the heartiest co-operation of British statesmen and British officials, which only represents the prevailing attitude in Great Britain of active sympathy with the full development of the other nations of the British Empire. This spirit of friendly co-operation has not been more finely shown than by the British Ambassador at Washington, Sir Esme Howard. The attitude of genuine helpfulness which has been practically and generously demonstrated by the Ambassador and the members of his staff, has been of very great service to Canada on the occasion of her entry into the diplomatic sphere.

One has heard it said that the entry of the Dominions into diplomacy will impair the diplomatic unity of the Empire and therefore may threaten imperial unity itself. Perhaps at first blush such misgivings may seem forgivable. When the proposal was first seriously made, seven years ago, it represented an entirely new conception—a new idea—and someone has said that "there is no pain like the pain of a new idea". But the unity of the British Empire rests not on machinery or on the absence of machinery, but on the faith and loyalty of the nations composing it. As for Canada, there is no true Canadian living who does not wish to see the Empire placed on an enduring basis and Canada's connection with it deepened and strengthened. The new development will not weaken the ties which bind the Empire together. I believe it will have the contrary effect. There are now in Washington three envoys of His Britannic Majesty—the British Ambassador, the Minister of the Irish Free State and the Canadian Minister. But the presence in a great friendly capital of these three representatives of the King, responsible to different governments of His Majesty, should provide not obstacles to unity but, I believe, bridges to an even greater unity between the British nations which these envoys represent. It is, after all, the human motives behind mechanism that really matter.

Canada believes in the Empire, and it is the wish of the Canadian people that nothing that exists to serve our national ends should operate to the detriment of the larger unity of which we are a part. The three British envoys in your capital represent a great peace-loving family of nations, united not only in friendly co-operation with each other, but united also in our friendship for this great nation to whose government we are now accredited. The modern British Empire is most illogical if you like, even paradoxical. But logic, fortunately, I think, has never had much to do with the Empire. The great thing is— and this will appeal to the practical mind of all Anglo-Saxons—it works! That is after all what matters most. A few months ago, just after the late Imperial Conference was over, I heard a British statesman say that in all his career, and it had not been a short one, the British Empire, in his opinion, had never been on a sounder or more enduring basis. I believe that he was right. I know that the British connection is a precious heritage treasured by Canadians whatever language they may speak, and is symbolized by our universal loyalty to the gracious Sovereign to whom we offer our homage.

I have spoken at some length of Canada's

relation to the great Commonwealth of nations to which she belongs. I do not think that
the subject is irrelevant. In the first place
I believe you are interested in it. I know
that you are well-wishers of that old Empire
and are glad to see harmony in her councils
and co-operation among her members, and a
resolve among them to give her an unshakeable future. And, again, you who know us in
Canada, and how many there are of you who
have a wide knowledge of, and a generous interest in our traditions—you who know us in
Canada are glad that we are happy in our
membership in the larger Commonwealth.
And you are right. The sounder our relations
are with the Mother Country, the sounder will
be those with the rest of the world. A man
who is loyal to his traditions, true to himself,
who has peace within him makes, after all, the
best neighbour. This is as true of nations.
Our national sentiment in Canada and our
attachment to the Empire of which we are
part, run side by side with, and even are an
aid to, our sincere and active friendship for
our only near neighbour. And this feeling,
let me add, grows stronger the better we get
to know their neighbour. May I say to you
gentlemen here to-night what a source of
genuine pride it is to me to be the first person

to represent my country diplomatically in yours. No British subject in the foreign service of his government could ask for a more congenial community in which to work than this great warm-hearted and hospitable land. I am touched more than I can say by the welcome I have received here and everywhere since my arrival. I appreciate its sincerity as I value the charm of its expression. I accept it, not as having any personal significance, but as a true compliment to the nation which I am privileged to represent. It will be my pleasure to tell the people of Canada that their envoy has received a welcome for which he will be ever grateful.

One word in conclusion: I thank you from the bottom of my heart for the honour I have received at your hands this evening. You have given fresh confidence to a new diplomat, who I shall confess has addressed himself to a very unfamiliar task. You have made me look forward with even greater pleasure to my sojourn in your midst. I shall one day leave my post content if, with your help, I shall then be able to feel that I have done something—it will indeed be all that lies in my power—to strengthen the bonds of sympathy between His Majesty's oldest Dominion and the government and people of your great Republic.

THE PRESS AND DIPLOMACY

*At the Annual Dinner of the
American Newspaper Publish-
ers' Association, New York, 28th
April, 1927*

Mr. Chairman and Gentlemen:

I deeply appreciate the honour of being
asked to address this distinguished gathering.
I can only say that I approach those mysterious powers that we call the Press with all
the humility that becomes the unitiated, for
I must confess, Mr. Chairman, that my active
career as a journalist was confined to two
episodes. In my old University of Toronto I
was one of the founders of a magazine which
died of pernicious financial anaemia, and later,
at Oxford, I helped to found another peri-
odical which expired, like so many student
journals, a victim of acute congestion of the
editorial column.

Let me admit this evening, sir, that in appearing before a body of gentlemen connected
with the vast and intricate organism of the
newspaper world, I am painfully reminded of
a certain country editor of whom you may have

heard. A cabled despatch was received in his office one day to the effect that the King of the Tonga Islands was dead. This seemed to him a matter of some importance, and it obviously called for editorial comment. But where were the Tonga Islands? Who was the deceased monarch, and who his heir? At last he hit on this moving passage—"The King of the Tonga Islands is dead. We hardly know what to say." Although I am at a loss what to say I am nevertheless encouraged by the fact that it is not only the experts—the publishers and editors—who are able to express views and opinions on the subject of the Press; there is another group in the community who possess a profound and expert knowledge of the subject, and who give generously and freely of their advice on the theory and technique of newspaper publishing. I refer to that important and significant body of human beings who cheerfully subscribe themselves at the end of their communications to the editor with the significant words "Constant Reader" or "Lifelong Subscriber". It is only by the authority conferred by membership in this body that I address you this evening.

The newspapers to-day, of course, are, in a sense that applies to no other institution,

everybody's business. The modern Press is
coterminous with civilization. One hundred
per cent. of the population of a great modern
state is now under the influence of the daily
newspaper. New types of journals have come
into being to serve a section of the public to
whom the older newspaper would be meaning-
less. Half the criticism which is levelled
against the newspaper of to-day is due to the
fact that, in the process of shaping itself to
meet the needs of the outer fringes of literacy,
the form and the content had to be altered
and popularized. An English statesman of
a somewhat die-hard cast of mind once com-
mented on the journalistic exploits of a contemporary—who shall be nameless—and in referring to the many pictures which one of his
papers was created to carry, he said gloomily
of its publisher: "not content with creating a
paper for people who cannot think, he has now
produced a paper for those who cannot read".
Adverse criticism of anything of course is
easy; criticism of any institution so close to us
as the Press is inevitable. I do not intend for a
moment to enter on the dangerous ground of
the controversy as to whether the newspaper
reflects or moulds public opinion; but it is
well to remember, whatever may be the negative or positive force of the modern news-

paper, that the Press of no community can run counter to popular feeling, and if we criticize the modern newspaper we must be equally critical of the civilization whose vagaries we require it daily to record for us, and for which civilization we each of us have our own measure of responsibility.

I wonder sometimes what a citizen of Mars would say of modern society, if he were to judge it by the daily papers, if they could be left on his doorstep by some new and disturbing invention, an improvement on wireless telephony or television—shall we call it tele-delivery? It might be gently suggested that the Martian would assume from the columns of his daily tele-delivered journal that his cousins on the earth were more troubled by domestic infelicity than is universally true. He might gather, too, that we were more unduly elated by picturesque forms of homicide than is habitually the case. He might be impressed with an observation which has been made to the effect that the news in some of our newspapers now and then resembles the character of Adam as he appears in one of the scenes of an old German play. In this drama Adam moves majestically across the stage on his way to be created, thus suggesting some of our modern "news" which, too, is of a slightly anticipatory nature.

As I have suggested, gentlemen, it would be an impertinence for me to make any observations about the state of the Press. The layman is amazed by the stupendous growth of the modern newspaper and the unbelievable efficiency with which it is now produced, (and in this development this country has played a brilliant part); but this great mechanical enterprise must not obscure from us the fact, for I believe it to be a fact, that the quality, too, of the modern newspaper is steadily improving, that the best newspapers of the world were never better or as good. In a striking address to a group of fellow editors, delivered by Mr. Whitelaw Reid, about fifty years ago, he forecast that the future of the newspaper lay in the attraction, on a greater scale, of first-class minds to its production. If you will permit a layman to say so, I believe that Mr. Reid's prophecy is steadily being fulfilled, and that not only is the circulation of the modern newspaper infinitely wider, but, through the brains which serve it, the product which is being circulated is of far higher quality.

I hope, at this point, you will let me say, with gratitude, that in establishing the new Canadian Legation in Washington I have received from no section of your great community a warmer or more sincere welcome than I have from the members of your profession. The generous reception which the men in the newspaper world have given to our new enterprise has contributed in no small degree to the genuine pleasure with which this new link of friendship between your country and mine has been forged.

I have said, gentlemen, and I have said it with a profound sense of truth, that I am, personally, little qualified to speak of newspapers or of the problems of newspapers. On the other hand, officially, I can be said to occupy almost a paternal relationship to the Press of your country. Your news may come from all quarters of the earth, the interpretation of that news from you yourselves, but the raw material on which that news and its interpretation are set out, comes, principally, from my country. I discovered, the other day, that the total newsprint consumed in the United States is just over 3,000,000 tons per annum. As newsprint, or as still in the form of pulp or pulpwood, just under 2,000,000 tons come in, each year, from Canada, and ninety per cent. of the newsprint you import is Canadian. Therefore, although you may not carry as much Canadian news as often

we can supply, and you do not invariably express the Canadian point of view in your edi-
torials, it can at least be said that two-thirds
of your newspapers have, in a practical sense,
a solid Canadian basis.

Such a form of export as I have mentioned
is but a symbol of the intercourse, social and
economic, which marks our common boundary
line.   Such contacts, of course, bring many
mutual blessings.   One of the chief reasons
why good relations between your country and
mine are permanent is that Canadians and
Americans, on a vast scale, have personal
knowledge of one another.   We feel at home
on your side of the border, and you on ours.
(In fact, we are so successful in making
visitors from the United States feel at home
that every summer, so I have been told, about
150,000 post cards are mailed in Canadian
letter boxes with United States stamps on
them.)

After all very few questions between individuals can resist a settlement when both
parties talk them over at a common table.   If,
when a misunderstanding arises between two
great communities, the public of each, along
with its Press, could be moved *en masse* over
the dividing frontier, each to learn the other's
point of view, there would be no international

problem. But personal contact cannot be carried out on such a vast scale; and the two
permanent agencies that can provide first-
hand knowledge and information, and the
understanding that is based on them, are the
institution which you, gentlemen, represent,
and the profession of which I have the honour
to be a new member. The Press and diplomacy, in the international sphere, share a
common task. It is sometimes urged that the
diplomat and the journalist have nothing in
common and cannot be expected to co-operate.
The professions, it is true, are different and
the goals are not the same, but I believe it is
true that there is a common ground and a common end to be served by both in the high task
of interpreting the minds of nations.

In the modern age, when a people can talk
to a people, the Press can be the unofficial
diplomat of democracies. The diplomat must
represent governments, the Press can represent the public directly. This popular diplomacy carries its own sanctions in the moral
force which it can exercise—the kegs of moral
gunpowder which lie in its power. When you
ask where the diplomat comes in, I may say
he often feels as though he were sitting on the
keg! But it surely is a truism that diplomacy
without the aid of a high-minded and well-

equipped Press is powerless to achieve its task of furthering a better understanding between nations. There is no sphere in which the Press has such an influence and power as in international relations. Of the events that happen about us the public can form its own opinion. But in the tangled, mysterious web of international affairs, our only sources of information are through the columns we read each day, and therefore, for both the news and its interpretation we must look to the daily newspaper.

The relations beween your country and mine are a veritable symbol of peace. I believe it is the conscientious aim of the Press of North America to deepen and strengthen this feeling of harmony and goodwill between our two democracies. With the same high end in view diplomatic relations have been established between Washington and Ottawa. Let us hope that this great partnership in a common cause between journalists and diplomats, between the envoys of peoples and the envoys of governments, may prevail throughout the world.

A NORTH AMERICAN EXPERIMENT

At the Twenty-first Annual Din-
ner of the American Society of
International Law, Washington,
30th April, 1927

Mr. President, Ladies and Gentlemen:

I am amazed at my own rashness in accepting your very charming invitation to be here
this evening, because I do not think there is
any picture of temerity more complete than
that of a layman rising to address a group of
international lawyers on any subject related
to international law. I am not sure, as a matter of fact, that there is very much left to be
said on this subject when I contemplate the
volumes on the shelves of any well-equipped
library under the title "Law, International".
But if there has been too much said about international law in the last three centuries we
can agree that there seems, on the other hand,
to have been too little done. Too often still,
as we know so well, the law of nations takes
second place to the law of force. We are
reminded of Mark Twain's observation about

33

the weather: that "everyone goes on talking about it, but no one ever does anything".

However, ladies and gentlemen, I want to assure you for your comfort that I do not propose to talk about international law to-night. Discretion is the better part of valour. It is also three-fourths of the virtues of a diplomat —if my much abused profession can be allowed any virtue at all. All I wish to do for a few moments is to make some observations about the relations between your country and mine, a subject I have very much at heart, personally as well as officially.

We should not be frightened by the words "international law". The phrase, it is true, seems to the average man remote and detached from reality. "Grotius" after all is not exactly a household word in North America and we do not hear "sanctions" and "sovereignty" discussed very frequently in the street car or at the golf club. But international law ought to mean something to everybody, because there is no subject in human affairs in which we should be more deeply concerned, for the ultimate objective of the subject which has occupied the attention of you gentlemen here for the last three days is nothing short of the welfare of the world. There is a race going on at the present time, if it can be called a race, between

two forces, one which would keep the earth a
jungle, and another which would give it order
and justice.   If the latter succeeds in over-
taking the former and we are saved from
future catastrophes such as we encountered in
1914, it will be just because this society and
other like agencies here and in Europe, more
numerous now than ever before, are trying to
teach human beings that the principles of
decent behaviour which we accept as governing the relations between individuals should
govern those between nations as well.

In North America we sometimes feel ourselves happily immune from the troubles which
beset the older continents.   But there is, of
course, no true immunity for we are living in
a shrunken world.   Contagion from disease
in the body politic we cannot escape.   We were
stricken once not long ago and we can be
stricken once again.   Therefore, it is folly
not to be interested in what is being done to
spread a wider knowledge of those principles
which, if they prevail widely and popularly
—because that is the only way they can effect-
ively prevail—will ultimately bring about an
understanding between nations, on which alone
peace can rest.

In North America we have our own achievements in international relationships of which

we can be reasonably proud. Sometimes we
have been so successful that the public is unaware of the mechanism which has been used
to keep our relations as harmonious as they
have been. Our intercourse over the invisible
line to which Mr. Hughes has referred is
so free, our dealings so pleasant, our relationships so amicable that the spirit of harmony between us has seemed sometimes almost automatic. It seems to me, however, that
although we can be proud of the unbroken
tradition of a century or more of peace in
North America, we must remember that we
have had certain advantages on this continent
which have been denied our contemporaries
elsewhere. For one thing we have plenty of
room in North America. There is an abund-
ance of natural wealth still to be dug out of
the earth for the peoples on both sides of the
line. Again, both have been spared the legacy
of strife and hate centuries old which beset
the peoples of Europe. When we reflect with
pardonable pride on our accomplishments in
peace, I think we ought to remember that we
have been allowed to start afresh in North
America. We have been permitted to develop
our own traditions governing the relations between us. It is easy to forget that the frontiers which exist elsewhere too often mark cen-

turies of religious conflict, racial aggression, dynastic rivalries—that the modern European is often an innocent victim of the sins of his fathers. I think, therefore, that when we speak about our peaceful boundary line in North America we should always remember that there is no background of religious warfare between the peoples of New York State and Ontario, or a feud between rival dynasties in Manitoba and Minnesota, or ancient antagonism between two warring races in Montana and Alberta.

The frontier, after all, is the test of international relations. In a famous lecture in Oxford, Lord Curzon once pointed out that "frontiers are indeed the razor's edge on which hang suspended the modern issues of peace and war, of life or death between nations". We now see efforts all over the world to re-form frontiers—to give them a better atmosphere. We have neutralized zones, demilitarized areas, equalization of armaments; but these expedients, well-meant though they are, are simply after all mere devices to check a disease the germ of which has still to be found, isolated, and destroyed. The cure of international disease, this internecine warfare in the family of nations, surely rests on a new mental attitude on the part of the ordinary

men and women who make up nations: the
new state of mind which it is one of the objects of a society like yours to bring about.

The boundary line between your country
and mine is not a "frontier" in the familiar
sense of the word. It is rather a meeting
ground between two friendly states. A border
so long and so complicated as ours is, must
nevertheless, as your president has suggested
this evening, have its full quota of questions
for mutual adjustment, like the questions aris-
ing between any two business firms in adjacent
areas. Ours is a unique boundary. To begin
with, it is the longest border line between any
two organized states. Twelve hundred miles
of it are represented by an arbitrary line
drawn across the prairies, and as many miles
run through a tangled skein of boundary
waters. The boundary is traversed by two
hundred and sixty rivers and streams. It
passes through one of the wonders of the world
—Niagara Falls. Water-power has made it
twice a wonder, just as the importance of other
great sections of this international line has
been increased by the artificial use of water
for industrial power and also by its use for
irrigation. Both industrial energy and agricultural development are now related closely
to our boundary-water problems.

The preservation of harmony in this complicated line which runs between our peoples has required thought and effort on both sides. The machinery which we have employed to solve our border problems has been so successful that I believe it provides in some cases— one can say this without risk of overstatement —an example to the entire world of how stubborn questions can be settled if there are common sense and goodwill on both sides. I am thinking of one international body, with which many of you no doubt are familiar, which was set up in 1909 to deal with questions of common interest to the United States and Canada. It embodies two or three basic ideas which, to my mind, make it of far greater importance than the general public at least has ever realized. To the man in the street the work of this International Joint Commission means almost nothing. I think it is a pity that it does not mean more. It is highly regrettable that we do not realize just how successful we have been in establishing this permanent piece of mechanism for the adjustment of mutual problems. We may well be proud of the fact that in the seventeen years of the Commission's existence, twenty-two cases have come before it of the most intricate and exacting nature, and that in every case the report of the Commissioners has been unanimous. That in itself is a tribute not only to its personnel from both sides of the line, but to the wisdom of Mr. Elihu Root and Lord Bryce who mutually devised this body and established it in the Treaty of 1909.

They incorporated some important principles in the structure of the Commission. In the first place there is the essential factor of equality. There are three members from each side. Another element contributing to the success of the Commission is the fact that its membership is permanent. This seems to me a most significant matter. When the members of such a body are permanent, they, through the intimate association of years can acquire a confidence in one another's detachment of mind and the Commission as a whole can approach its problems, not as "ex parte" advocates but as a judicial body considering them on their merits. The creation of the International Joint Commission was a fine achievement, but if any one is stirring restlessly in his seat in mute and helpless anticipation of a layman's account of the Treaty of 1909, let me assure you that I do not propose to give you a dissertation on the articles of this Convention. Let me make just a few brief observations on the importance of what it did.

A writer in your own *Journal of International Law* a number of years ago pointed out that the act of the treaty which set up this Commission gave us "a permanent tribunal between Canada and the United States to which any questions or matters might be referred and decided by the principles of law and justice". In other words, we were given a "miniature Hague Tribunal" of our own. Under one article of the treaty any question may be referred to the Commission by the consent of both parties. Its powers are as wide as the powers of a body of this kind can be. But the Commission has thus far confined all its decisions to matters relating to the problems of our waterways. It approaches these problems in accordance with certain fundamental conceptions. First, it operates on the principle that the navigation of all boundary waters shall be forever free; secondly, it is laid down in the Convention that no diversion or obstruction that affects the flow of these waters shall be permitted without the consent of the Commission.

There is a provision in the Treaty of 1909 which I believe is practically unprecedented in international conventions. This extraordinary clause provides that if any action in connection with the levels or flow of boundary

waters should be taken on one side of the
boundary which injures, or is alleged to injure
a party on the other side, that party may take
his case into a court on that side of the line
on which the injury is alleged to have taken
place.   In other words, the resources of American and Canadian courts are pooled for the
benefit of the people on both sides of these
waterways.   Observations have been made
from time to time by statesmen to the effect
that if such a body had been in existence with
reference to the problems on the Danube or
the Rhine or other international waters in
Europe, many troubles and difficulties might
have been averted in that continent.   It is
difficult to refute this contention.

There is romance in many of the cases which
have been dealt with by the Commission, just
as much romance as in cases which have been
settled by a more picturesque but less peaceful form of arbitrament.   I am thinking of
one irrigation problem in the west of our respective countries of which some of you may
know.   On such questions the Commission has
final decision without appeal.   In Montana
there are two rivers which take their rise in
the foothills of the Rockies.   One is called the
St. Mary River and the other the Milk River.
The St. Mary River crosses the international

line in Canada and, like so many welcome
visitors from your side, stays there. The
other, the Milk River, is more fickle. It
crosses over the boundary and then returns
ultimately to flow into the Missouri. That
part of North America is a semi-arid region.
Water there is more precious than gold. There
was a great deal of difficulty about these particular streams. Dams were constructed, irrigation ditches were dug, levels of streams
were interfered with. It was thought wise
that in the Treaty of 1909 itself there should
be embodied the principle that the waters of
these two rivers should be regarded as one.
Under this provision a canal was ordered to
be dug and the Milk River and the St. Mary
River connected. I suppose, sir, this is the
first case of international relations where the
dilution of "milk" contributed to the welfare
of both sides. But that did not settle the
matter. There was a great deal of difficulty
with regard to this irrigation question because
there were two interpretations of the treaty,
and that is where the Joint Commission came
in. The Commissioners for a time held their
sittings somewhere in the east and carefully
studied the matter, but still the trouble continued and became more disturbing and extended in its effect until the Commission, like

a workmanlike body, finding it could not get the people to come to it to tell their difficulties, went itself to the people. An atmosphere of confidence was created, technical difficulties were overcome, and that question at least was erased from the current roster of international problems.

So much for one piece of mechanism which has operated to the mutual advantage of your country and mine. I think it is worth while sometimes to quote a concrete example to prove that when we are talking about good relations between Canada and the United States we are not speaking purely in terms of vague generalities. We are able to point to this as well as to other definite and successful efforts to maintain harmony over our international border. However, sir, the mechanism in such matters is less important than the spirit which animates it. If we preserve good will and harmonious relations and see them expressed between us in countless ways, it is because there is a spirit amongst the respective people of these two countries which creates and demands a feeling of goodwill. After all, law, international or municipal, in order to function must be based on human consent. Otherwise, it remains simply a pious aspiration. And if we have and always will have

perpetual concord in North America, whatever may be the form of its expression,
treaties, commissions, and even after-dinner
speeches, sir, it will rest on the belief which
prevails amongst the peoples north or south of
the 49th parallel that it would be a very foolish thing indeed if we could not get on well
together. We are good friends. Why? Not
because of protocols or treaties, but because we
share a spirit of neighbourliness and common
sense and a desire to know each other and to
understand each other's point of view, which
makes us, as far as amity between two nations
can be concerned, a happy and harmonious
international family.

The problem, after all, let me say in conclusion, is primarily an individual one. It
is the individual's point of view in these matters which ultimately counts. The problem
of international understanding, like all other
problems of civilization, therefore, is a matter
of education. Education is the path to
the solution of this question as to all others
in human affairs. Thanks to organizations
like your distinguished society, existing and
working now in Europe as well as in America,
this education is proceeding. Such education
must be a practical matter. The researches
of theoretical students of international law

must be supplemented by the efforts of practical experiments of international law. In the religious world there is an organization with which I am familiar which gives as one of its objects: "To spread the gospel without preaching it." We are all painfully familiar with efforts to preach the gospel without spreading it; but spreading the gospel without preaching it is a refreshing idea which may be well applied even to the subject of international law. There is a practical form in which this gospel of goodwill between nations can be preached by individuals. The understanding which exists between human beings who appreciate each other's point of view is a comparatively common thing but it only requires a little imagination to extend this to embrace not individuals but the groups of individuals which we call nations. It is through such a process that we can look for a real deepening and strengthening of understanding in the international world. And, ladies and gentlemen, it will be the pride of both democracies of North America if the concord which our two peoples enjoy will widen and extend until men, wherever they may live, will find what we have found here—that there is nothing incompatible between being patriotic citizens and good neighbours as well.

THE UNIVERSITY
AS AN INTERNATIONAL LINK

*At the Annual Commencement
of the University of Kentucky,
30th May, 1927*

Mr. President, Ladies and Gentlemen:

It is a great pleasure to be here to-day.
This is not only my first visit to the University
of Kentucky, it is the first time I have been
in your great state, although I have read of
your limestone hills and your lowlands with
their beautiful stretches of blue grass and the
fine race of men and women which they have
produced, from Daniel Boone and the
pioneers, and Henry Clay, to the Kentuckians
of to-day. Of these I have already had the
privilege of meeting a number since taking up
my new work. And I am very happy indeed
to be able to see something of Kentucky itself.

Now, ladies and gentlemen, this is the open
season for Commencement addresses. Perhaps I may put it this way: it is the open
season for that form of oratorical sport in
which itinerant sportsmen like myself are invited by hospitable game wardens like your

47

president to empty a few boxes of cartridges into a selected covey of carefully preserved game like yourselves. And here you are; you cannot escape. I have you at my mercy. The only hope I can give you is that the cartridges I am going to fire at you may be harmless blanks.

It is the greatest pleasure to me to be back again in the atmosphere of a university, where I always feel at home. I spent six years as an undergraduate, four in my old University of Toronto, and two in the ancient University of Oxford—and this was long enough to enable me to acquire a wholesome attitude of condescending tolerance towards my instructors, together with an affection for the undergraduate friends whose academic lot I shared. Then to redress the balance, I became an instructor for a few years, and instantly of course developed a healthy and profound contempt for the vacuity of the undergraduate mind!

However, ladies and gentlemen, what I did learn was this, that a college is composed not simply of the teachers and the taught but rather of a body of men and women, some older than the others, it is true, a few with greater experience than the rest but *all* bent on learning, in exchanging their ideas, in pursuing their path towards that mysterious goal which we call truth. A college in its true significance has been finely called a "corporate fellowship of intellectual adventure"—a community of professors and students engaged in a common quest, learning together and teaching each other too, for I think that it is just as absurd to suppose that the thoughtful student has nothing to teach, as it is to imagine that the man who has taken his degree has nothing more to learn. On the latter point at least, I think we can all agree.

Your university represents a fine tradition. The history of the University of Kentucky reveals in a high degree two outstanding characteristics of institutions of higher learning in this great country. In the first place, in its origin it represents that passionate belief in education which is surpassed nowhere else. Your university, although not founded until sixty odd years ago, is the lineal descendant of those schools which were built by the pioneers while the axe was still heard in the virgin forest. Your forefathers believed that material foundations were only built on sand without provision for the development of mind and spirit. And therefore, education was to be at the disposal of all. That has remained one of your great ideals.

It is a far cry from the days when the

student in Lexington pursued his way to college in danger of being scalped by the Indians before he reached the end of his journey, to the present comfortable age when the only risk lies at the end of the four years academic journey—that of being academically scalped by the professor. But I do not believe, although the days of physical pioneering are over, that the spirit of the pioneer is gone from your university. A hundred years ago, the margin of *cultivation* was being pushed westward. The process has long been completed but now under the leadership of this foundation and of its graduates all over the state, the margin of *knowledge*—of intellectual cultivation—is being steadily pushed forward.

This suggests the other great product of American education which is the creation of the state university, a family of which yours, here in Kentucky, is a distinguished member. The state university is the most characteristic educational development in America. It represents the state, the government, acting in a capacity unheard of a century ago—by which it assumes responsibility not only for common school education and even secondary education, but higher education itself; and in great institutions undertakes not only to develop the highest standards in practical activities but to disseminate its knowledge broadcast direct to the community as a whole, and also to act as an intelligence branch of government itself.

The university nowadays has come to mean many different things. You have broadened the meaning of this word in your country until the term can now conjure up a vast organization guiding the studies of many thousands of students, distributing knowledge direct to all who seek it—individuals, municipalities, business corporations—and dealing in all branches of human endeavour from Greek philosophy to municipal engineering. It presents a fine picture—this great engine of modern knowledge which you have created in so many places.

In contrast to this ultra-modern university, there are, carrying on their work here and there in your country, colleges of the old simple type whose task is still limited to the primary function of training the mind and character of the individual. Of course no university, however vast and complicated its system may be, can abandon this function, because it represents the very core of education.

The concentration on the individual student has remained the major concern of the two older universities of England. You are of course familiar with the conception. Its aim has always been to give the undergraduate a symmetrical development, to train his character, to give him a sense of responsible citizenship which is imparted in some measure by his membership in a closely-knit collegiate community. In mental training the great object is to teach the undergraduate to think straight. The body is by no means neglected but exercise is encouraged, not as an end in itself, but as a means to an end. This conception of education is not concerned so much with the acquisition of learning as with the knowledge of how to apply the learning which is acquired. The equipment which liberal education requires is simple. Men are regarded as being no less important a medium than books, for we often learn more from our fellows in an intimate community than from the printed page, and the excursions into books themselves under this system are made in the close companionship of the resident tutor whose personality counts for so much. Education in these ancient ivy-clad colleges which may seem so remote from modern affairs is after all a very practical thing because the learning it imparts is closely related to life. Perhaps that is why Oxford and Cambridge have been for so long a nursery of statesmen.

When one comes to Scotland the university

is different again. There the familiar picture
is one of hundreds of students flocking to the
inspiration of a famous lecturer. It would
perhaps not be unfair to say that Scottish
frugality breaks down when it comes to lectures. But the lectures in Scottish universities are of a high standard and the reverence
for philosophy, in the real, pure sense of the
word, the passion for learning and the contempt for what is felt to be irrelevant command our admiration. I wonder how many
student libraries can live up to the austere
standard set in the library of one undergraduate club which I visited once, in a great Scottish university. My guide, a senior member
of the university, waved his hand at the
shelves and turned to me with pride illuminating his face, and said "There's no' a seengle
freevolous buik in the entire collection!"

When we move to the Continent of Europe
we find the university almost exclusively concerned with the intellectual life, thinking little
about affairs outside the classroom but intensely interested in developing brains and producing thinkers. The greatest characteristic of
the continental universities perhaps is that
belief in pure research which has caused them
to lead the world in so many spheres. Why?
Because so often in poorly-equipped labora-

tories, in distant corners of Europe men have pursued their quest after abstract scientific truth with no desire for a short cut to some practical end and with no interest in letting the world know what they are doing, but have let research lead them whither it would. Their contribution to physics, chemistry and medical science tells its own story.

You may ask yourselves what sort of universities have we in Canada? Our universities, like Canadian life in general, show many streams of influence. Our older colleges are based on English and Scottish models. In Quebec, the universities have much in common with the colleges of France of the old régime, and our provincial universities have points in which they resemble those controlled by the governments of your states. But in our universities as in everything else in Canada we are developing characteristics which are ours. The strands in the fabric may be English or Scottish or French, but the pattern can be called Canadian.

I have suggested some of the qualities of universities in various countries. They are very different in form, but does this mean that the university stands in the way of international concord? Far from it. I think the contrary is true, and if there is one idea which

I ask you to carry away with you to-day it is
that universities everywhere should be a great
unifying force between nations and that men
and women in this university world of which
I speak should be the first to help to promote
a better understanding between them.

Let me tell you why I think so. In the first
place, in the university there is a concentration of knowledge. Discord between nations
like most of the disharmony in life is due to
ignorance. If one nation knew at first hand
something of the other's problems and difficulties—I am not referring only to the statesmen, but the general public to whom the statesmen must, in a democracy, be responsible—
we should see concord between nations. In a
university community such knowledge is most
likely to exist. I remember a conference in
my own university at Toronto a few years ago,
held by a student organization, at which there
were present several hundred students from
all over the Dominion, and in addition to them
some sixty to seventy representatives of other
countries, races and continents. It was one
of those meetings which take place in universities which are intended to set right the
wrongs of this troubled world. (I believe as
a matter of fact that the ideas expressed at
such gatherings have, frequently, an effect be-

yond even the enthusiastic beliefs of those who
utter them.   There is no greater dynamic in
the world than an idea.)   I remember at this
gathering as the subject turned, as it often
did, on international questions, that the
presence of representatives from so many diverse and often conflicting nationalities gave
a reality to the discussion and a renewed
understanding to all who participated of the
difficulties involved.   And, as so often happens on such occasions, an open-minded search
for truth pervaded the gathering.   Those taking part unconsciously tried to live up to the
advice of Sir Walter Raleigh, the late Professor of English at Oxford, who said "Judge
if you must but at least first try to understand".   I have tried to suggest one function
which a university can perform in aid of better
international understanding.

The universities of your country and mine
perform a unique service in international concord by the exchange of personnel.   The movement, it is true, is more southward than north-
ward.   There are a great many hundred professors from Canada on the teaching staffs of
your universities and colleges.   But to offer
a balance to this there are hundreds of Canadians with doctors' degrees won at your universities teaching in ours.   Such an exchange

is wholesome because it means an exchange of ideas, and, provided we select the best ideas for importation both ways, the exchange is of mutual benefit.

This brings me to a third point. Universities, even those which exist under different flags, cannot be competitors in a material sense. Friendly rivalry there can be, and should be, but universities wherever they are, are essentially bound in a holy alliance against ignorance of mind, disease of the body and all the obstacles which beset the advance of natural science. There is nothing finer than that freemasonry of mind that unites men, however divided by race or language, as long as they are labouring in the sphere of thought. You go into the ante-room of a great surgeon and you will find on the walls the photographs of his heroes from all countries. If you enter into the library of a great scholar you will find that his intellectual allegiance transcends all national bounds. There can be no customs tariff, no physical barriers against ideas. When Frederick Banting, a member of my own university, made the discovery which conquered one of the diseases which have been the scourge of society, the results of his researches encircled the globe, until now in every country the sufferer is benefiting from the

quiet years of work spent by Dr. Banting in
his laboratory in Toronto.

There is one more point. It is not only
through knowledge, the exchange of personnel,
through the confraternity of minds that universities can provide a link between the nations of the world. There is something beyond that. You will remember that in the
middle ages universities spoke a common language. In those great informal unorganized
groups of teachers and students—in Bologna,
Paris, Oxford—the current language was
Latin. That was the international currency
of educated men. There is still a common language to-day. It is not Latin, because I am
afraid that if we were limited in our conversation nowadays to the tongue of Virgil and
Cicero we should most of us be a silent folk,
but there is a language of common understanding which ought to be the possession of men
and women privileged to remain for a few
years in a community whose very aim it is to
understand the meaning of what its members
see around them.

After all, what is it that you take away
from a university when you leave it? What do
you carry away with you after the four years
you spend within its walls? A degree? A
symbol only, but an important symbol of what

your community has given you, what your instructors have done for you as your guides
through these critical years, and what you
have done for yourselves in developing your
minds for the work you are to follow. Friend-
ships? Nothing finer as a possession. General knowledge? Vastly important for whatever you do in after life. Special training for
a vocation? Essential for whatever profession you elect to follow. But none of these
represents the most significant gift you carry
away with you from your university. The
most precious endowment you receive within
these walls, it seems to me, is a state of mind.
Let me suggest the qualities which this state
of mind should possess. It should be liberal,
dispassionate, curious and humane. By liberal, I mean fair, unprejudiced; by dispassionate, intellectually honest; by curious, men-
tally awake; by humane, sensitive and kindly.
Such a state of mind as this will help us to see
life in its true proportions, its true shades.
Cardinal Newman once said that a liberal education enabled one to see a pattern in what
otherwise was a garish medley of coloured
threads. Somewhere in this strange mass of
colour and line we call the world, there is a
scheme for us to find. Do you know the lines
which John Masefield prints at the end of his

play "Pompey the Great"? If you do, you
will remember the scene that closes the play.
Pompey, his dreams turned to ashes, lies dead
on the Egyptian shore, while his ship with
its blood-red sail slowly puts out to sea, and
the poet says:

> Blindly and bloodily we drift,
> Our interests clog our hearts with dreams.
> God make my brooding soul a rift
> Through which a meaning gleams.

Ladies and gentlemen, it is the privilege of
the universities in your country, together with
the universities in my country, whose greetings I bring you to-day, side by side to carry
on their quest after that *meaning* in the world
which it is their task to seek, and to make their
common contribution to that understanding
among nations which is peace itself.

THE COLLEGE AND THE COMMUNITY

*At the Annual Commencement of
Swarthmore College, Pennsyl-
vania, 6th June, 1927*

Mr. President, Ladies and Gentlemen:

It is the greatest pleasure to me to be with
you here to-day and back again in the atmosphere of a college. My own roots are struck
fairly deep in academic soil. To return to it
now and then is a genuine privilege. I hope,
ladies and gentlemen, that such visits paid
by outsiders to academic communities do no
lasting damage to the undergraduate body; on
the other hand, I am quite sure that they con-
fer permanent benefits on the visitor. For one
thing, you will be glad to know that it makes
him feel humble. There is a quaint superstition current to the effect that a man who moves
in what we complacently call the practical
world—the world of affairs—has passed beyond the need of education—that his function
in education, if any, is to teach. We say that
such a man can speak with the wisdom of experience. Well, he may speak with wisdom or
he may not, but I know that his experience is

more likely to make him wise if he carries with
him and manages to preserve that spirit which
it is the privilege of just such an institution
as yours to bequeath—the spirit of open en-
quiry and a true sense of values, and the balanced judgment which a liberal education
exists to impart.

To come into your midst makes the ageing
visitor feel like an undergraduate once
more. (I admit that this is a rather dangerous
experience for one who is supposed to be a
sober and responsible diplomat.) Dangerous,
but most pleasant, for during the years you are
in statu pupillari you are, I was going to say,
irresponsible, but that is not the word. Let
me rather say "inconsequential". You are not
irresponsible, because you have a solemn responsibility to develop an intellectual curiosity, a passion for truth and a willingness to
follow it, wherever it leads, wherever it asks
you to go in the curriculum or (I hope the
Faculty won't object) *outside* the curriculum.
I don't think, as a matter of fact, that professors can ever object to the wayward digres-
sions of an eager student—intellectual de-
tours on the road to an examination—because
with the growth of intellectual curiosity will
grow the student's reverence for learning itself and for the great profession under whose
guidance he works.

It is, of course, very easy to say that a liberal education is a search for truth and then to avoid the embarrassing necessity of defining truth itself. But the definition of truth in its various forms is, after all, the task of education. Its aim should be to teach us to see truth on all sides of a controversy. Truth is to be found in some measure on both sides of most conflicts, for most controversies in life are not between abstract right and abstract wrong, between black and white. Life is more subtle than that. Human nature has a natural weakness for false antitheses—for artificial issues. It is one high function of the college to teach us to reduce the barriers, to bridge the gulfs in this world which so loves to divide itself—if you will allow me to mix my metaphors—into isolated compartments, water-tight and idea-proof. And it is therefore the more important that there should be no gulf between the college and the community —between the world of action and the world of ideas. For there is no antithesis between ideas and acts, words and deeds—they are complementary. Sir Walter Raleigh—not the Raleigh of Elizabeth, but the Raleigh of George V,—once said "a word is a deed, and problems of expression and conduct can never be wholly separated". Ideas and actions are,

of course, interdependent. One provides the
force for the other. Ideas are the dynamic to
action and action without ideas is like a ship
with neither engine nor rudder. Ideas are
after all the most powerful things in the world.
They are not quoted on the stock exchange
along with cotton and rubber, but a few sets of
ideas capable of being written on a sheet or
two of paper have, after all, divided the world
into the three or four great religions which,
for centuries, men fought for as for their lives.
A group of ideas is the rock on which this Republic rests. A few ideas give to the British
Empire its enduring strength.

Therefore, it is well to visit the home of
ideas when one may. Such contacts are not
beyond the needs even of the practical man.
We worship the word "practical" nowadays.
But what is a practical man? Disraeli, in one
of his novels, says that "a practical man is one
who practises the errors of his predecessors".
That is a hard saying. But we can at least
agree that whether we are practical men or
impractical men, we are less likely to practise
the errors of the past or fall into errors in
the future, when we maintain an open-minded
belief in ideas and the places where they are
held in greatest respect.

In some religious communities, a custom

exists by which men—lay as well as clerical—
can now and then enter a "retreat"—a temporary retirement from the distractions of
modern life, from its insistent crowds, its
strident mechanism which so often we complacently allow to master us—and in an atmosphere of detachment and serenity can readjust
their sense of values. The plan might well be
extended, so that the men whose task it is to
act might keep in touch with the men whose
privilege it is to *think*. The wiser the man
the easier such contact. The greatest men I
have known have been those in high office—
and such men often attain to such places—
who have preserved a respect for ideas. This
carries with it a reverence for youth. How
many ideas have been started on their mysterious careers by students in their glorious
freedom, who light-heartedly took the uni-
verse to pieces as a watch is taken to pieces
without the embarrassing obligation to put it
together again?

But if the gulf between college and community is sometimes wide, I believe the fault
is more often upon the academic side. The
college has two foes, the philistine and—I am
grateful for the man who coined the word—
the "highbrow". The philistine is ever at the
gates but the highbrow is a traitor within the

walls.   The philistine is wrong but honest; the
highbrow is wrong and also false to the very
gifts with which he has been endowed. Someone has said that the highbrow is a man "whose
education has outstripped his intelligence".
Perhaps this is true.   The highbrow possesses
knowledge without understanding; he presents to the world a spurious learning, an af-
fected mannerism with no relation to reality.
He lacks the simplicity of the scholar.   He
lacks the ardour of a student.   And he is responsible for two-thirds of the philistines of
whom he—and never the real scholar—com-
plains.   The modern college stands on the one
hand in danger of "highbrowism"—pedantry
—the form of erudition which bears no relation to reality; while, on the other, is the constant peril which we encounter when the remorseless activity of life to-day is too strongly
reflected in those communities that should be
islands of thought in a sea of movement—reflected in swollen curricula, labyrinthine examinations and in all the inexorable mechanism
which is, of course, a means and not in itself
an end.

On the world of the college rests the responsibility of understanding the larger world
which it serves, and of keeping contact between the two—the real personal contact which

alone can suffice. I can think of one concrete
example of a successful effort to maintain
such a relationship. In my old university at
Toronto, there is a debating society in which
the affairs of our nation are discussed (and
settled) at intervals throughout the academic
term. It was the desire of the committee to
follow the example of the undergraduate
Unions of Oxford and Cambridge and induce
active men of affairs to come—not to talk to
them, but to debate with them. This year,
their ambitions were realized—and incidentally, the record of the older bodies outstripped,
(because I do not believe these had ever enter-
tained the head of a government in office)—
when the Prime Minister of Canada came and
took part in a debate with the students, on a
motion which involved the policy of his government. The debate was conducted on traditional parliamentary lines, was earnestly and
seriously carried on by all participants, and
brought to a division in which the five hundred
students present gave their decision in a free
vote. A few weeks later, the Leader of His
Majesty's Opposition took a similar part in
a debate on another subject. These occasions
I think have a genuine significance because
they symbolized a healthy relationship between the practical experience of politics on

the one hand, and the study of politics on the other, which can only extend and deepen to the advantage of both.

A few years ago, in a remote corner of this country, I visited what was left of an ancient religious community which had flourished for a century or more, and had preserved its own peculiar faith. A remnant of the congregation remained, as unconscious of the world that passed to and fro on the highway a mile away, as might be the monks of Mount Athos. We were shown the place by one called the Eldress Sarah, who had lived for forty years in the same room and at the same task. She said that before we left we must see Brother William, for it was he who was the head of this little community and whose guidance had kept it together in the years of its decay. "But," the Eldress said, "you may not find him in. You see Brother William writes hymns and often he goes to the top of a hill to 'get in line' again." I suppose it is not too fantastic to suggest that the college is a hilltop in human affairs where one should be able to "get in line", as the old Eldress put it, with truth in its various forms, and whither even those beset with workaday problems can go now and then for intellectual refreshment. For it is from such a hilltop that one can get the detachment that gives perspective.

You may know the charming legend of the Florentine painter Uccello, who lived and worked at the time when the early primitives were growing tired of painting two-dimensional landscapes, and were learning to put depth into their pictures. Happy in the knowledge of what relative size and the device of converging lines could do to his work, he awoke one night and exclaimed to his wife: "How sweet a thing is perspective". This is what we need in every-day affairs, and that is what the college exists to give us: a sense of perspective, a sense of proportion, a sense of relative values—the ability and the will, in the painting of every-day life, to depict that thing small and remote because it is trivial and unimportant, and this thing large and in the foreground because it is essential. It is not for me or anyone else to say what should be drawn large and what should be drawn small. That is for you to decide for yourselves.

Do not let us limit this sense of perspective to the hours when we work. Let it cover the hours when we play. The college, after all, is not concerned only with the preparation for one's vocation, the earning of a livelihood. A liberal education should give us the knowledge of how to live—in leisure and in work.

There is something, for instance, in the pursuit of a well-chosen hobby—in leisure intelligently spent—that keeps a man's sense of proportion, his sense of values. It may not always add to knowledge but it does something greater, it increases wisdom. It will help one to see one's work in a better perspective. My advice is, choose a hobby, or rather let a hobby choose you, because a hobby is the natural expression of your own character, as your college and you develop it. It may be gardening, or collecting prints, or horses, or writing plays, or chemistry, or binding books, or architecture, or climbing mountains, or astronomy, or fishing in the summer (which means thinking about fishing in the winter), or theology, or golf (or anything except talking about golf), but, whatever it is, you will be the better for it. Your work will be the better for it. Therefore, find your hobby and ride it hard. You will never know whither it may carry you or how far it may bring you on the road to truth, or along whichever of the converging roads to truth we choose to travel.

You may know the verses written about an Englishman too little known—George Wyndham—who rode his hobbies straight and well, who worked hard and played hard—who lived

not a long life but one that was both broad and
deep:

> He held his soul with both his hands,
> And bound it by a thousand strands
> To Truth and Beauty.
> Then wove the story of his days,
> A warp of Love and woof of Praise,
> A web of Duty.

This is a picture of one who had lived a
balanced life with a symmetry of growth and
something of the sense of values which a college exists to impart.

Ladies and gentlemen, in the quest after
true values which we all pursue in common,
yours is a highly privileged community, splendidly equipped and finely led. You are the
heirs of a noble tradition. There can be no
finer background for the intellectual life. The
gentle faith in which Swarthmore was born
possesses a wise serenity of mind and innate
peace, and yet a spirit of progress which never
confuses inertia with calm. Above all, you
have the legacy of that great-hearted friendliness which made your Founders and their followers too, in the full measure of the word,
the Friends of Men.

THE MAKING OF A NATION

*Lecture on the Alumni War
Memorial Foundation at Milton
Academy, Massachusetts, 30th
November, 1927*

Headmaster, Ladies and Gentlemen:

It is a great honour to be with you here and I am deeply conscious of the privilege which you have given me. There is nothing that can make quite the same appeal as a great school —one that has preserved that indefinable thing called tradition. You have a fine tradition here in Milton—carried on now for one century and a quarter. But you do more than maintain your old customs. You are creating new ones, and this foundation under which I come to you to-night, established by way of tribute to those Miltonians who laid down their lives in the Great War, is a new tradition in the making.

What a wise memorial it is! I am happy to participate in it—grateful for what I have learned from you in the last two days. We cannot more fittingly honour the dead than by quickening our own minds and hearts—

we that survive them—by recalling that chal-
lenge pictured on your beautiful memorial
tablet with its words, "The cause shall not
fail". Our Canadian soldier-poet put the same
thought in the mouths of the dead in battle
when he wrote:

> To you from failing hands we throw
>   The torch; be yours to hold it high.
>   If ye break faith with us who die
> We shall not sleep, though poppies grow
>   In Flanders fields.

I am glad to be with you to help to do honour
to those sons of Milton who did not return
from the war. I count it a high privilege to
be the unworthy successor of the distinguished men who have already visited Milton
upon this foundation.

As to my choice of subject this evening, I
ask you to be charitable. You may, however,
count it as not unnatural that a Canadian
Minister should wish to talk to you about Canada. I do not propose to inflict upon you a
lecture on Canadian economics, or geography,
or even Canadian history. What I want to
do—not, I hope, at too great length—is to
give you some idea of how Canada grew from
a few scattered hamlets of French and Eng-

lish settlers in the primitive "bush" into that
something which we call a nation.

A nation, of course, is hard to define. But
perhaps it is not worth while to trouble about
definitions. You who live here as citizens of
your own great country know without juggl-
ing with words what it means. You have a
pride in your nation's past, belief in its present, and confidence in its future. You are prepared—and this is the real test—to make
sacrifices for it. Your nationality is a thing
big enough to inspire devotion on the part
of the individual and to demand co-operation on the part of the community. We in
Canada have developed over the years our
own spirit of nationality. It is of this that I
want to talk to you.

You are now passing through a period in
the history of your country when you are
celebrating the anniversaries of the great
events, the battles and historic meetings, that
mark its beginning one hundred and fifty
years ago. It happens that Canada, that is
to say Canada as a British country, has also
just a little more than a century and a half
behind it. The history of the United States
as an independent country dates from 1776.
Civil government under the British flag in
Canada began just a few years before this.

To-day finds us neighbouring nations, but the road we have travelled has been strikingly different. The years 1776, 1783, and 1789 mark the rapid steps by which you achieved, almost in a single bound, complete sovereignty. Our nationhood was developed in slow, measured stages extending over a century and a half. You put an end to the political structure which we may call the first British Empire. With the lessons of history in mind, it has been possible for Canada, in working out its own destiny under the British Crown, to take its part in laying the foundations of a new British Empire on true and enduring lines.

The old Empire, with its colonies governed by one Parliament in Great Britain, was built on a simple system. It was strictly logical, but like so many logical things it failed. The new Empire to which we belong has preserved many of the forms of the old, but the spirit has changed. It is no longer represented by a "Mother Country" with "infant colonies" round her knee. Nor is it even suggested by a mother with grown-up daughters. The picture now is that of a group of partners — Great Britain and the Dominions — members of a sisterhood of nations. Through the years there has been created, by the countless acts of statesmen in Great Britain and overseas, that which has come to be called a Dominion. The old-fashioned historian, if you told him that a state existed which was entirely free, and yet not independent, which owed allegiance to a King across the water, and yet possessed complete self-government, would say, like the countryman who saw his first giraffe, "There ain't no such animal"; and yet such a state is a fact— just as much a fact as a monarchy or a republic. And it was in Canada that this strange new thing called a Dominion was developed, not because any group of men sat down and said to each other, "Let's start something new", but because, over a period of a century and a half, a community, beyond your northern boundary, steadily widened the range of self-government as necessity arose and practical problems had to be faced and solved.

You will know from your own history books some of the main points in our story. I shall not talk of the heroic age of the explorers. That is a golden tale in itself. The voyages of the first discoverers, Cartier, Champlain, and La Salle, and the men they inspired; La Vérendrye and his sons discovering the prairies and spending twenty years in that gallant search for the Western Sea which was brought to an end by the mountains which they found across their path; Sir Alexander Mackenzie, who fifty years after daubed a proud legend on a rock on the Pacific shore— "From Canada [and that meant from Montreal], by land, 1793." And then there were the splendid failures like that of Sir John Franklin which thrill us just as much as success. We Canadians have a warm place in our hearts for this race of adventurers. We are still hearing that call of which Kipling tells—the "voice as bad as conscience" which says to us:

Something hidden. Go and find it. Go and look
    behind the Ranges—
Something lost behind the Ranges. Lost and wait-
    ing for you. Go!

In our great, vast country we are still exploring, not now through lake and over portage only, but by aeroplane as well, to find terminals for new railways that are nosing their way through the wilderness, and harbours for ships that have still to be built, and to make surveys for the homes of unborn Canadians.

Let me begin my sketch in 1759. In that year, you will recall, a great Englishman, Wolfe, met in battle a great Frenchman,

Montcalm, in the fields near Quebec, and in a short and gallant fight replaced the lilies of France with the Union Jack of Britain. This battle between French and English was fought with the chivalry of a gentlemen's duel. Whenever you visit Quebec, if you look for the monument of Wolfe and Montcalm, you will find inscribed on its base one of the most stirring and fitting inscriptions ever chiselled in stone:

Mortem virtus communem, famam historia, monumentum posteritas dedit.
Valour gave them a common death, history a common fame, posterity a common monument.

What was to be done by Great Britain with its newly won possession? In those days the conqueror as a rule was none too nice in his care for the feelings of the conquered. But wisdom and justice finally prevailed in the counsels of the time and to the sixty thousand French people living in Canada were guaranteed those precious possessions, liberty of worship and freedom of language. Thus was promise given of just treatment for this old community under their new flag.

Of the country itself in those early years what picture can I give you? One writer of the time politely described it as a place "fit only to send exiles to as a punishment for their misspent lives''. So little value was attached to this newly found land that in 1758 and 1759 there had been a persistent clamour to force the government, in the settlement of the treaty after the long war with France, to abandon Canada altogether and accept in its place the tiny island of Guadeloupe in the Caribbean Sea. Guadeloupe is six hundred square miles in area. Canada, although it seemed then little less than a wilderness of forest and snow, has grown to cover 3,700,000 square miles. And yet political wiseacres of the day gave the sage counsel, ''Keep Guadeloupe; let Canada go''. It is an interesting fact that the best pamphlet pleading that Canada was worth more to the Empire than any sugar island was written by Benjamin Franklin.

Let me pass quickly by some milestones. In 1791 comes a turn in the road which is worth examining. After the peace of 1783 was signed, many thousands of people moved from the new republic into British North America. In their new home they were called ''Loyalists''. They settled by the sea, and north of Lake Ontario, and they endured with quiet heroism untold rigours in their new and arduous life. Although they had taken the

royalist side in your great struggle, these
people did not believe in autocratic government. They believed in local self-government
as strongly as John Adams himself. In fact
the Englishman—the Anglo-Saxon—wherever
he is or whatever he does, or whatever uniform he wears, has a stubborn, unconquerable
love of personal freedom and liberty. So it
was not long before these newly settled refu-
gees demanded popular assemblies in Canada
like those which they had left behind them
and which their kin already enjoyed in the
Maritime Provinces, just as insistently as
their revolutionary friends had protested
against the taxation of Grenville and North.

This demand was answered, and 1791 finds
us in the beginning of a new era in Canada.
Upper Canada (now Ontario) was established
as one province with a few thousand English-
speaking settlers, and Lower Canada (now
Quebec) was set up as another province on
the banks of the St. Lawrence, with a larger
population, chiefly French. Each had its
Assembly, each its Governor, and each its
nominated second chamber or Legislative
Council. The grant of representative institutions to French and English alike was vastly
important to the future of the Empire. It
made clear, as students of our history have

pointed out, that British liberty and British rights were not to be enjoyed by inhabitants of Great Britain and their descendants alone, but were to belong to all those who lived under the Union Jack and who were equal to the responsibilities involved.

One of the most picturesque scenes in our history, to my mind, is the opening of the first Legislature in Upper Canada, by Colonel Simcoe, the Lieutenant-Governor, when the majestic pageantry of Westminster was as faithfully reproduced as was possible in a building of logs in a clearing in the bush. The creation of popular assemblies in these two provinces of Canada was a great step. The farmer and the fur-trader now elected their representatives to voice their grievances and their aspirations. But 1791 does not represent the solution of a problem. It marks the beginning of a long and stormy controversy. Why? You have heard the old riddle, "What happens when an irresistible force meets an immovable object?" Such a combination had existed in the Thirteen Colonies before the revolution. The irresistible force had been the popular assembly and the immovable object was the Governor, acting on orders from Whitehall. As a matter of fact, in most essentials, the government of the Canadas in

1791 presented the same problem. A Governor was instructed to govern. A popular
assembly was elected to legislate. When the
Legislature—Assembly and Council acting
together—passed a bill which the Governor
thought was exceeding the proper limits, he
could reserve it or refuse to assent to it. Or—
and this with graver consequences—he could
play off his nominated Council against the
popular assembly and make it carry out
his wishes by rejecting bills. The obvious
result was the refusal of supplies by the
Assembly.

The first possession of a nation, like that
of an individual, is the control of its own
affairs. The first half of the nineteenth century marks the struggle in the Canadas for
this right. The world outside was little interested. To the casual observer it seemed
simply a political quarrel—the endless argument between the "ins" and "outs". Sometimes there emerged the figure of a Governor
applying his instructions from home with too
little imagination; sometimes the stage was
occupied by citizens with a zeal for self-
government. But what was the real meaning of this endless controversy? It was actually a renewed and final debate on the question: "Can a colony govern itself and still re-

main in the British Empire?'' In 1776 you,
in this country, had answered this question
by a resounding "No". Was it possible for
the people of British North America to say
"Yes"? Most of those concerned in the controversy probably did not know the importance of what they did. They were interested in practical questions, the control of the
appointments of judges and surveyors, the
voting of funds, the division of public lands,
and other issues which need not concern us
now. But the principles involved meant more
than they knew.

In 1837, as the girl queen Victoria ascended
her throne, armed rebellions broke out in
both Upper and Lower Canada. Sixty years
before, thirteen British provinces had taken
up arms against the Crown—now two more
were following their example. Did this mean
the end? The rebellions were easily crushed,
but they were symptomatic of the spirit of
discontent which remained. The government
at home decided that the whole situation
should be fully explored and sent out as
Governor of the Canadas the first Earl of Durham. Durham was an extraordinary figure.
He was an aristocrat of the aristocrats, im-
perious, vain, aloof, impetuous. No one perhaps could be less democratic, as we often

use the word nowadays—he brought out to
Canada a great retinue, including a band of
music. But not every democrat wears home-
spun and Durham was not called "Radical
Jack" for nothing. He understood the essentials of democratic government. He also had
three great qualities which so often have char-
acterized Englishmen of his class: a vivid
sense of public duty, keen political insight,
and the courage of his convictions.

Lord Durham's "Report on the Affairs of
British North America" is probably the greatest state paper in British colonial history.
If the Declaration of Independence is the
foundation of your nation, Lord Durham's
"Report," presented to Parliament in 1839,
is the corner-stone of the modern British Empire. Why? Because it set down the political
truth that in a colony the Crown, or its representative the Governor, must submit to the
necessary consequences of representative institutions. Durham's "Report", gathering up
the "broken colonial aspirations" and giving
them the dignity of a great name, ultimately
altered the whole theory of colonial government. But this change did not take place overnight. The Provinces of Upper and Lower
Canada were united in 1841, as Durham had
recommended, but four Governors came and

went before the principle of responsible self-
government was fully accepted. In England
the tradition of public service in great families
is strong, and it is therefore not unnatural that
it should have fallen to Durham's son-in-law,
Lord Elgin, to establish finally the principle
of responsible self-government in an episode
which nearly cost him his life. In 1849, a
measure to compensate those who had suffered
losses in the rebellion of 1837 was passed by
the Canadian Parliament at Montreal. The
bill had aroused furious opposition by those
who claimed that it would involve payment to
rebels. Violent scenes took place. The Parliament buildings were burned. Elgin was as-
saulted in the streets. He was determined to
give the royal assent to the bill because it had
been passed by a majority in the Legislature.
His own views he held to be of no account.
The vice-regal signature on this bill is the
symbol of colonial responsible self-government. History gives us a great roll of heroes
who have helped to make nations. But I
think that the Earl of Elgin, emerging from
his carriage with a two-pound stone in his
hand which had been hurled at him because he
insisted on acting according to the will of the
majority, presents a figure that might well
take its place amongst the champions of dem-

ocracy. All that has developed since this
episode by which the Dominions have acquired
the control of their affairs, in the external as
well as in the domestic sphere, simply marks
the extension of one principle. This principle
is best represented by Lord Elgin's unfalter-
ing assent to a measure which had been passed
by the majority of the people's elected representatives.

The issue of self-government had been
sternly contested, on the one hand by patriotic
British North Americans and statesmanlike
Englishmen who believed that the way to keep
British North America in the British Empire
was to give it the fullest possible control of its
affairs, and on the other by men on both sides
of the ocean—no less honest—who believed
that self-government would mean the end of
the Empire. Why? Because, as they reasoned, the Governor, if he must act in accordance with the popular majority, might be
forced to act in a manner contrary to his instructions from home. He could not serve two
masters. And this view had been held in British North America as well as in Great Britain.
It is well to remember that this was not a
quarrel between England and the colonies. It
was an argument between two schools of
thought which were represented both in the

Mother Country and overseas. In the controversies between Great Britain and the colonies this has always been the case. I need
not remind you of the championship which
your cause received, one hundred and fifty
years ago, at the hands of Chatham and Ed-
mund Burke.

The question of responsible government in
my country has now been settled for seventy-
five years and more. It took courage on the
part of British North American statesmen
and vision on the part of their colleagues in
Britain to take the step; and, great as it was,
it is a striking thing that this change was
brought about by no revolution, nor by the
adoption of a new constitution, nor by the
abolition of any office, nor by anything even so
slight as a change of words in a public document—although, of course, the instructions
given to the Governor-General changed as the
colony grew and developed. Executive power
still, in fact, remained in the Governor's
hands. He could still, theoretically, refuse
assent to bills or he could reserve them for the
consideration of the imperial government if he
saw fit. But a new principle had been established in men's minds. Something which is
called *constitutional right* began to assert itself in 1849 in concrete form, and to place

definite limits on *legal power*. This conflict between constitutional law and constitutional right occurs often in British political history. It has been two centuries since a British sovereign has refused assent to a bill passed by Parliament. The legal power to do so technically still remains, but the constitutional right of the democracy to make its own laws has existed for so long that the royal assent is given as a matter of course. This is the characteristic British way of dealing with constitutional development.

I have talked about this growth of responsible government at considerable length. I make no apologies because it marks the most important step on the road to nationhood. It not only was important for British North America, but was of vital significance to the whole British Empire. On what became Canadian soil, the experiment was worked out of harmonizing responsible colonial government with membership in a great Commonwealth. As self-government grew, attachment of the colony to the larger unit was not weakened, but rather strengthened. It was found possible to reconcile nationality and imperial unity despite all the melancholy prophecies of those who thought it could not be done, and, as it became increasingly successful, other self-governing states grew up within the Empire, like Australia, New Zealand, and South Africa. The whole Empire was built anew round this corner-stone of national liberty and the very word empire came to have a new and different meaning.

I have illustrated our national developments from two important phases in the early history of British North America: the one commences with the establishment of British institutions and closes with the creation of representative government; the second, the natural outcome of the first, is the long process covering fifty years or more, which led to the acceptance of the principle of responsible cabinet government in the middle of the last century.

May I touch on the third and fourth great periods, which might be said to complete the story? One of these was ushered in by what we call Confederation—the great period during which British North America was unified, enlarged, and developed, and acquired its final stature. And the fourth period covers the last twelve years or so, commencing with the tragic romance of the Great War. This placed the keystone in our national arch and gave Canada, in addition to national *stature,* national *status.*

Of Confederation I shall say but little. This year we are celebrating the Diamond Jubilee of this event. Much has been said about its meaning. Before 1867, what is now the Dominion of Canada was broken up into several scattered communities operating with no common government—the original Canada (now Ontario and Quebec, united before 1867), the three provinces by the sea, and, beyond more than two thousand miles of almost unbroken wilderness, the settlements on the west coast which are now British Columbia.

If self-government is essential to a nation, so is unity, but unity in British North America in the early 'sixties seemed a distant hope. The problem is shown by the confusion of the currency. In the Canadas the pound and the dollar were both legal and in active competition. In Nova Scotia you could purchase commodities in Peruvian, Mexican, or Colombian dollars as you liked. Communications were sadly deficient. If you wished to travel between Toronto and Winnipeg (or what is now Winnipeg), or between Winnipeg and Vancouver, in winter, or between Montreal and St. John, you had to pass from British soil altogether. A letter from Toronto to Vancouver would probably go by way of South America. More serious than these physical difficulties were the administrative, political, and financial problems, which would make too long a story to be told here. A group of great men, however, as has so often happened in your history as well as in ours, was not lacking to perform a great and necessary task. If you should happen to visit Ottawa you will find on Parliament Hill statues bearing the names of Sir John Macdonald, George Brown, Sir George Cartier, and others who had the vision to see in their minds' eye a single country under a single government extending from the Atlantic to the Pacific. One of these Fathers of Confederation, as we call them, said in a prophetic speech (and in the style of his day), that he could see "one great nationality bound like the shield of Achilles by the blue rim of ocean". But it took men of vision to breathe the word "nationality" at all in reference to these scattered people (in number, only four-fifths of the present population of Massachusetts) who were taking possession of half a continent, larger in extent even than your own vast country. It required practical men, too, to work out the problem. In doing so they borrowed from you that great federal principle which had worked so well in this country, which leaves the states (provinces we call them) free to look after their own domestic affairs, but which places the whole population for national purposes under the control of a central government. But our central government itself was modelled as closely as could be done on the government of Great Britain, for Canada is really a constitutional monarchy.

In the creation of the Dominion on a great national scale, Great Britain did all she could to help. British statesmen of the day fully shared the faith of the Fathers of Confederation in the future of the new Dominion. The Secretary of State for the Colonies, Lord Carnarvon, who introduced into the House of Lords the measure which created modern Canada, expressed himself in terms of wise British statesmanship when he said:

> We are laying the foundation of a great State— perhaps one which at a future day may even over- shadow this country. But, come what may, we shall rejoice that we have shown neither indifference to their wishes, nor jealousy of their aspirations, but that we honestly and sincerely to the utmost of our power and knowledge, fostered their growth, recog- nizing in it the conditions of our own greatness. We are in this measure setting the crown to the free institutions which more than a quarter of a centui ago we gave them, and therein we remove, as I firmly believe, all possibilities of future jealousy or misunderstanding.

On July 1st, 1867, by a royal proclamation the modern Canada came into being with its four original provinces—Ontario, Quebec, Nova Scotia, and New Brunswick. The original name suggested by colonial statesmen was the "Kingdom of Canada", but it was thought that the term might lead to misunderstandings, and the picturesque story is that one of the Fathers of Confederation came to the council table one morning and made his contribution to the search for a name from a passage in the Bible: "He shall have Dominion from sea to sea and from the river unto the ends of the earth". But it was only in men's vision that Canada reached from sea to sea until this result was achieved after six years of effort, during which British Columbia joined the union and the province of Prince Edward Island, in the Gulf of St. Lawrence, also entered it. During this period too, that vast area known as the North West Territories was acquired from the ancient Hudson's Bay Company, which had been founded two centuries before by Prince Rupert of England.

But let me pass to the fourth and final phase of this national growth. Canada acquired a personality in the nineteenth century and physical growth came with it. Something else was needed to create direct touch with the world at large, and this came with the Great War. What was the effect on Canada of this war which made nations and destroyed empires? A country with less than nine millions of people cannot engage in four and a half years of conflict and send four hundred thousand men to serve in France with the King's colours, of whom sixty thousand gave their lives, without gaining a more vivid consciousness of what lies beyond its shores.

With the war, Canada "swung into the full current of the world's life" and established relations with neighbours near and far. It was, therefore, appropriate when the great peace was signed at Versailles, in 1919, that Canada, along with the other Dominions which had fought by her side, should have the right to place her own signature on the document. When the League of Nations was created, it was fitting that these units, which had entered the war as nations, should enter as nations, too, that society of peoples that came into being to make war more remote. (A further step was taken when Canada this year became a member of the executive body of the League—the Council—and this with the blessing of the representatives of Great Britain.)

And so a process has steadily gone on in

which a new and revitalized Empire—a third
British Empire, also called, and appropriately, the British Commonwealth of Nations—
has emerged. If the war destroyed some
political structures, it transformed and created anew that of which Canada is an integral
part, giving it greater unity and strength because it rests on the full development of its
component parts. That is why the Dominions,
if they wish, can establish diplomatic relations
with foreign countries, why, for instance, Canada has set up its legation in the capital of
your country, and why you have reciprocated.
(And here let me thank Milton Academy for
sending to Canada, as the first foreign Minister to be received by the Dominion, a most
distinguished graduate in the person of Mr.
William Phillips.)

I think it was Lord Salisbury who said,
"The looser the tie, the closer the bond." The
paradox is true. The touchstone of the British Empire is liberty. And that is why the
British Empire is dynamic and not static, why
the Great War, instead of destroying its fabric as it did in the case of four historic empires, left ours stronger than ever before.
But you may ask: What are the bonds between the Dominions and the Mother Country? First of all, there is the great symbol of

unity embodied in the Crown. The King of
England is also the King of Canada, of Australia, of New Zealand, and of the other Dominions. Every executive act of these great
states is done in his name. Every member
of Parliament takes the oath of allegiance
to His Majesty. Every commission is issued
and all government property is held in the
name of the King. The Sovereign who oc-
cupies the throne not only represents the
spiritual unity of the Empire, but also the
national life of each Dominion in it. For the
Crown, as every one knows, is not only a
jewelled object to be seen behind great bars
in the Tower of London. It is much more.
When I see on one of the mail waggons in
Canada the Royal Crown, with the letters
"G.R." on each side of it, it never fails to stir
my imagination. It suggests so many things.
It conjures up an unbroken stretch of a thous-
and years and more of history. It suggests the
coherence of a great Commonwealth, covering a quarter of the area of the globe, and
containing one-fourth of its people. And it
also represents the nationality of Canada and
of each country within the Empire, of which
the monarch who wears the Crown is the national sovereign.

But there is something else that unites our

Commonwealth. There is a common citizenship. An Englishman or a Scotsman coming
to Canada requires no naturalization. After
a short residence he becomes a citizen auto-
matically, with all the privileges of citizenship. On the other hand, a Canadian or Aus-
tralian going to England enjoys the same
rights as the other British subjects who were
born in that country. He can vote, can even
stand for election to Parliament.

Then there are those great indefinable
bonds of common traditions and common institutions which we share with the people of
Great Britain, not to speak of the countless
ties of family and race which mean so much
in human affairs. And above all there is that
great community of feeling and interest which
gives to the British peoples a unity enduring
and indivisible.

Our nationality and our orientation are
well expressed by the coat of arms which we
have chosen. The ancient stock from which
Canadians have sprung is represented in the
quarterings by the lions of England, the lilies
of France, the lion of Scotland, and the Irish
harp. The new nationality made up of these
elements is marked by the three maple leaves
which have become the special emblem of Canada. The shield is supported by those tradi-

tional heraldic beasts, the lion and the unicorn, which can be said to stand for the British institutions which all Canadians inherit. Surmounting the whole is the British Crown, the mystical symbol of the Empire's unity and of the sovereignty to which Canada owes allegiance.

I have tried to tell you something of the Dominion's story. Burke once said that a statesman is required to have "a disposition to preserve and an ability to improve taken together". Somehow it seems to me that in Canada we have, unconsciously perhaps, tried to hold such a balance. We have tried both to improve and preserve. We are a mixture of new and old. We have a new nationality with an ancient allegiance. It is a strange, illogical structure, this British Empire of 1927 in which our young nation is a loyal partner. Lawyers sometimes find it difficult to understand. It is not easy to pigeonhole. Textbooks have to be rewritten to describe it. But it has been planted foursquare on the solid stones of the liberties of young independent-minded nations, and if the sceptic says, How can it be? how can this liberty and unity be joined together? one might well reply in the words with which an Englishman once answered a sceptic, by quoting the line from Goethe which can be translated: "Him I love who attempts the impossible". One might add that he who attempts the impossible with faith not seldom achieves it.

Through the years, therefore, the bonds of affection which unite us to our sisters in the British Commonwealth have grown stronger as our sense of nationality has deepened. At the same time there has been strengthened the concord which exists between the Dominion and its great neighbour to the south. Canada, like your country, has passed through its period of trial and stress. No human being or human institution can accomplish much without the lessons of endurance and steadfastness. There is a famous passage in the works of the poet whose name this school bears, which speaks of the future of the state in words which have the grandeur of organ music. I like to think that your northern neighbour has shared the poet's prophecy with you and all those who have kept true to their heritage, and that we, in Milton's words, can "outlive those pangs and wax young again, entering the glorious ways of truth and prosperous virtue, destined to become great and honourable in these latter ages".

THE COMMON HERITAGE

Before the New York Branch of the English-Speaking Union, at a Dinner in Honour of the Canadian Minister, 16th December, 1927

Mr. Chairman, Ladies and Gentlemen:

I greatly appreciate the honour of appearing under the ægis of the English-speaking Union of the United States, and am glad to share even in this small way in its activities. The present day world is full of newly formed movements and organizations. One of the effects of the war which, I believe, is a promising by-product of that catastrophe, has been the wide-spread creation of new associations of human beings united for the purpose of prosecuting the ideas in which they believe sufficiently to work and make sacrifices for. Such bodies operate in all directions. There are those which concentrate, here and there, on national security and development. Others abound which think in terms of international co-operation and amity. But of all the human causes which men serve, there is, to my mind, none nobler than that object to which you have been dedicated since your incorporation: "To draw together in the bond of comradeship the English-speaking people of the world". I say there is no cause nobler than this, and, I also believe, no cause more enduring and no cause, in the long run, more impervious to disparagement from without or from within our respective communities.

We call the American and British Commonwealths, when we refer to them jointly, the "English-speaking" world. It is hard to find another applicable term. The phrase Anglo-Saxon, for instance, not unnaturally draws an indignant protest from the Celt. Strictly speaking, the term English-speaking is, of course, a misnomer. We do not all speak English. I am not now referring to that exuberant idiom in which, for instance, the reports of baseball games are chronicled in the daily Press. This has its own virility and charm although it cannot be said to resemble closely the standard of Johnsonian prose. I refer rather to the fact—not always remembered— that in the British Commonwealth there are three millions of people of French or of Dutch descent who speak the languages of their own forbears; and that the Legislatures of three of the British Dominions sanction the use, as the official language of debate, along with English, of the French, the Irish or the Dutch tongues.

Nevertheless, the term "English-speaking" is perhaps not inappropriate as applied to the peoples of the United States and the British Empire. Not only because, of course, it represents the language of the majority—the five millions of people who spoke English in the days of Shakespeare have grown to 200,000,000 to-day. But the term is appropriate for another reason. If English is the language of the majority, those minorities who do not speak it enjoy the free use of their own tongue, because of those ideals of liberty of which the English speech for centuries has been the vehicle. I like to think that all peoples within this English-speaking world of ours who possess such rights as those of language and religion, too, enjoy them for this reason: that certain conceptions of society have been held and transmitted and diffused throughout the world by the people to whom Shakespeare and Milton and the English Bible have been a common heritage.

The effect of a common language is of course immeasurable. Language is not only the expression of a people's mind; it can influence the mind itself. When it is called, as it often is, the soul of a people, the sentiment is not mere empty rhetoric. It is a vitalizing organic thing—not only created but creating. Peoples who speak the same tongue cannot differ greatly in their conceptions. They may disagree—argument is the privilege of kinship—and when they disagree, they are more audible and comprehensible because of their common language. But they cannot differ on the fundamentals—on the basic things of life —because language is inseparable from the ideas which it incorporates.

A language, to unify and harmonize, to possess vitality, must, however, be the unconscious outcome of centuries of human experience; it must have grown. It cannot be manufactured. Those persons who dream of a universal idiom forget what language really is. Perhaps some day we may have some mechanical linguistic system for utilitarian use, but it cannot be a language. The wisest comment I ever heard on one of the made-to-order languages whose use is being propagated, was this: "You can't pray in it; you can't make love in it; you can't swear in it". One might add "you can't make a joke in it". The manufactured language is beyond the pale of human emotion.

On such an occasion as this, it is natural
to think of those things which the English-
speaking peoples share along with their common tongue. There are, for instance, the ties
of kinship existing between us. Perhaps it
is possible to over-emphasize the bonds of
common ancestry as a unifying force. The
maxim, "Blood is thicker than water" may
be true, but the common ideas which the English-speaking peoples possess, whatever their
racial antecedents, are the strongest bonds of
all. Of all the ideas which our two peoples
share, and there are many, the greatest is that
conception of human liberty which is deeply
imbedded in the fabric of both the Commonwealths. It was that passion for freedom
which gave birth to this great country a century and a half ago. The structure of the
great Empire of which we, in Canada, are
citizens, shows just as graphically the idea
of the liberty for which men of British stock
have always stood. It is our foundation stone
no less than yours. The British Dominions
possess within the generous bounds of their
Commonwealth, and in allegiance to its throne,
a freedom perfect and complete.

This evolution of self-government within
the British Empire has taken place, through
the generations, largely on the soil of the

nation which is your northern neighbour, and
commenced at about the time when you at-
tained your nationhood. If language is the
touchstone of liberty, it is interesting to recall
that the first step in the long, slow process by
which a self-governing Dominion was created
was the granting, by an English-speaking
power, of the freedom of language, and also
the liberty of religion, to those 60,000 French
who comprised the population of Canada when
the lilies of France were replaced, in 1763, by
the Union Jack. And then over the years,
step by step, practical problems being solved
as they occurred, the conception of a free self-
governing Dominion was worked out. Not
through any break with the past, nor any
change in sovereignty, but by a reinterpreta-
tion of existing institutions. Wise statesmanship in both the colony and the Mother Country believed that self-government, in the fullest sense, was possible within the Commonwealth, and so it was. And the British Commonwealth gained in unity and in strength by
the full growth of the nations which comprised
it. And now you, and we in Canada, and our
sister Dominions, and the Mother Country
which is the cradle of these ideas, are trustees
of a great legacy of rights and privileges and
liberties which we cherish not only for the

good of ourselves, but for the world at large. There is nothing more characteristic of our common inheritance.

There is another conception which the American and British peoples cherish with equal earnestness and conviction—a love of peace. We believe that war as a settlement of disputes is tragically futile—as futile as the personal duel which common sense, in our countries a century ago, relegated to the limbo of obsolete things. What a tragedy that men will still appeal to force collectively when they have long since learned to submit individual differences to the arbitrament of reason! We have a symbol of our love of peace here, in North America, in the dividing line between your country and mine. This historic boundary not only marks the meeting ground between Canada and her great neighbour, but also the line between your country and the Empire of which we are part, and is the perpetual symbol of the peace between them. There certainly is nothing very warlike about this boundary, nothing more martial than a customs officer here and there. The sentries left a century ago, and if guns remain they belong to museums, not to arsenals.

Mr. Root has said that "the indispensable prerequisite of a lasting peace is the creation

of the international mind". Perhaps we need
a definition of the international mind. It does
not, of course, mean the mind of those who are
the friends of every country but their own.
Nor does it refer to those who regard nationality itself as a menace to peace. It would be a
colourless world that had no place for the diversified national traditions and cultures that
give richness and variety to life. One great
enemy of society, in this mechanical age, is the
standardization which threatens to reduce personalities to a common type. Let us welcome
national differences within our English-speaking world as well as outside of it. It is well
that, here in North America, we have two
countries side by side, each approaching the
problems of civilization in a manner true to itself. We may learn much from your achievements. You are good enough to say that our
experiments are not without value to you. The
cosmopolitan ideal is at basis a watery conception of life. The international ideal of
goodwill between nations presupposes the existence of self-respecting nations consciously
living their own life. International friendship has no relation to international uniformity. It is possible to be a good patriot and a
good neighbour too. The international mind
might be described as the mind which, with a

firm belief in its own country, can project itself into the problems of the others and see
and understand their points of view. International concord is essentially a thing of the
mind—of the spirit. In reference to the relations between the American and British
peoples, one often hears the phrase "hands
across the sea". It is hard to know quite what
this means. But if it means alliances, tangible
links of any kind, let us beware of it. Material
bonds may tend to divide. Spiritual ties can
only unite. For *hands* across the sea, let us, as
has been well said, substitute *minds* across the
sea.

Serious misunderstanding is impossible
within the English-speaking world. From
time to time its units may differ. There is
security in the very candour with which we
express our views in this common tongue
which we can all understand. We have only
to keep a true perspective and the differences
which may occur will show their relative un-
importance beside our common interests and
common obligations. Not only is real misunderstanding between our two peoples impossible, but it is significant that even on those
two occasions, now happily distant a century
and more, and never to recur, when armed
hostility did exist between us, the ties of kin-

ship were never forgotten. The only wars between the English-speaking peoples were really civil wars. They never interrupted social intercourse between the nations. As everyone knows, the Norfolk squire, Coke, represented an important element in Great Britain, when he boasted that he had drunk the health of George Washington every night until the peace of 1783 was signed.

Just outside the town of Princeton there is a grave which encloses the unnamed bodies of a group of British and American officers and men who fell in the battle at that place just over one hundred and fifty years ago. On a great stone has been chiselled four lines written for the purpose by the English poet, Alfred Noyes. They read:

Here freedom stood, by slaughtered friend and foe,
And ere the wrath paled or that sunset died,
Looked through the ages; then, with eyes aglow,
Laid them, to wait that future, side by side.

We are now living in the future forecast in these verses. A century and a half after these men fell, troops in British and American uniforms have met again on American soil, this time in friendship to take part in a common ceremony commemorating a common action. On Armistice Day, a few weeks ago, took place the dedication of the simple monument which your government graciously permitted us to erect in your national Valhalla at Arlington, to mark the gallantry of those fellow-citizens of yours, who fought and gave their lives in our army in the Great War. On this occasion, the soldiers from each nation took part in a piece of symbolism as real as it was impressive. It was a memorable scene. As the two great flags, the Stars and Stripes and the Union Jack, parted and revealed the great granite cross, and the sound of the Last Post was heard on the trumpets, your Guard of Honour and our Guard of Honour presented arms in silent salute. Then when the prayers had been said and the hymns sung and the simple addresses given by representatives of both countries, our band played the Star Spangled Banner and your band played God Save The King, and the troops of both nations, British and American, marched off the ground in a single column. I believe that that scene expressed a truth that lies deep in the hearts of the people of both the British Commonwealth and of your great Republic.

EDUCATION
AND THE BALANCED LIFE

*Commemoration Day Address,
Johns Hopkins University,
Baltimore, 22nd February, 1928*

Mr. President, Ladies and Gentlemen:

As a Canadian I have peculiar pleasure in
a visit to Johns Hopkins and this for several
reasons. For one thing there are many personal ties which link this university with those
of my country. Before our own graduate
schools commenced to develop strength, many
Canadian students found their way, and some
are still glad to come, to Baltimore to enjoy
the privileges of your great schools for ad-
vanced studies. Some of these have stayed
to take their place among your teachers, and
I hope it may not be regarded as unbecoming
if I say that Canada is proud of the men of
learning who have represented, and still represent, the Dominion in your distinguished
faculty. Johns Hopkins demonstrates the
truth that amongst the many services—un-
assessed and unassessable—which the university can render to society, is that of providing

a community where men of different nations can meet as scholars in a common allegiance to learning which is in no sense in conflict with their varying loyalties as citizens.

There is one name upon the roll of Canadians who have passed through your halls to which I cannot help referring—that of Sir William Osler. His fine biography by Dr. Harvey Cushing (another great name brilliantly associated with this university) has served to bring out with renewed force the qualities and the stature which all of us who knew him, knew he possessed. Osler had developed in a rare degree characteristics which it is the business of a university to impart: a passion for learning and with it the enthusiasm which learning could not quell, and an intense pursuit of his own branch of science, but not so intense as to cause a neglect of the humanities. He possessed, too, a deep affection for his own country, attested by the bequest of his great library to his old university, McGill. But his fine patriotism was never allowed to narrow his conception of human life as a whole, for the plane on which live the Oslers of the world transcends international boundaries.

Osler died as Regius Professor at Oxford, and we can regard his work in England as being a contribution made by your university, as well as by those of Canada, to the enrichment of science and learning in the Empire of which Canada is part. You have had many points of contact with British scholarship through the years. These began with the liberal action of your first president in inviting the English scientist Huxley to deliver the address on the foundation of the university, fifty-two years ago. And those who believe in the profound significance of Anglo-American understanding, and endeavour to strengthen it, will not forget that in your halls Walter Page received part of his preparation for life. I am glad to think that there is now a permanent foundation within this university bearing his name and dedicated to the concord between our peoples for which he did so much.

When one thinks of the Johns Hopkins University, one thinks at once of the unique contribution which it has been your privilege to make to higher education. It is not inappropriate that your own corporate festival should fall on the birthday of the founder of your nation, for the importance to your national life, and indeed to the world at large, of what was demonstrated in the establishment of Johns Hopkins, cannot be measured. The happy union of large-minded generosity with imagination and intellect here in Baltimore in 1876, carried into effect a view of a university's function which, according to the opinion of such an observer as Lord Bryce, had never been put into practice in America or in Great Britain before. For here was established not simply a group of buildings labelled "University", with the life within still to come—the form awaiting the spirit— nor merely a body of youths pursuing their studies under the discipline required by immaturity—nor simply a group of departments giving the *ad hoc* training leading to a profession. All of these things, good in themselves, have been added to your activities, but Johns Hopkins makes its contribution to the world primarily in that free, untrammelled search for truth on which it embarked at its foundation. Benjamin Franklin put this question to the candidates for election to his little society: "Do you love truth for truth's sake, and will you endeavour impartially to find and receive it for yourself and communicate it to others?" There could be no better test for an institution of learning. It was a great achievement when, in this foundation, you put this into brilliant practice; and, partly due to your example, the North American uni-

versity in the last two generations or so has
added to the great function of teaching, that
of systematic thinking performed, as it were,
as a corporate act.

On occasions of this kind, it is a familiar
failing of a layman privileged as I am to-day
to enjoy an hour or so in a pleasant and hospitable atmosphere, to convey gratuitous information on the function of universities to the
learned men who are responsible for their
operation; to make unsolicited observations
on the product of universities for the benefit
of the innocent alumni who may be within
hearing; and to impose unprovoked advice
upon the helpless undergraduate who may be
marshalled in front of him without a chance
of distraction or a hope of escape. But the
layman must be conscious of the decent re-
ticence which becomes his position in the presence of those who know far more of the functions of a university than he. He is, after all,
dealing with an ancient institution whose principles are immutable. It seems to me, however, that the widespread consideration which
is being given to-day to university problems
is not inappropriate. An organism which has
grown so fast as the modern university and
has been equipped so lavishly with men and
tools, creates new problems by reason of its

very efficiency. The magnitude of the machinery with which we are endowed can be as much of an embarrassment as the size of our task.

What a place the university has come to occupy in the modern community! It is no longer a retreat where a privileged few can find an esoteric learning, but an institution influencing the entire community not only indirectly, through the quality of its graduates, but directly as well. It has assumed new corporate importance. Its researches have an intimate relation to the community in all branches of life. Its knowledge is brought to bear on every department of public affairs, business, agriculture, engineering, no less than the older professions. The education of all is dependent upon it. A small percentage of men and women may earn its degrees, but the educational standards of the entire community are set within its walls, where are taught the men and women who teach the teachers of the common school. The university, in brief, represents the place which we give knowledge in modern life, and for this reason, if for no other, we may well honour it along with religion and the state as the third member of a triad to which our devotion is due.

Our problem with the modern university

is not, however, to recognize its virtues, it is rather to prevent an unbecoming competition amongst them—to find among them a pervading harmony. Perhaps one can go further and say that however complicated may have become the task of the university, we must still regard a sense of harmony, of proportion, as one of its finest legacies. The problem of balance, of course, offers fewer difficulties in the realm of liberal education because the very essence of the latter is harmony. The symmetries of undergraduate life should be easy to maintain in that pleasant world of books and sport and clubs. Yet when I look at some of the universities I know, it seems none too easy to find men graduating from them with that balanced development which is surely not an unreasonable objective of undergraduate training. The substance of such an education might be said, without being unduly exacting, to include in right proportion awakened intellectual curiosity, the enjoyment of recreation as a means to an end and not an end in itself, and the gift of understanding men. We produce fine scholars, sound athletes, and good fellows in plenty, but how often one part is played to the neglect or the exclusion of the others. Perhaps we can place some of the blame upon modern civilization. I wonder if

the world ever needed the familiar counsel of
the old Greek tag μηδὲν ἄγαν—nothing in ex-
cess—more than to-day. Is it just fancy that
makes a balanced existence seem increasingly hard to achieve? Society seems to love
to attach labels to classify us, and to insist
that our classification be not disturbed by in-
consistencies. We are asked to stay on our
proper shelves. The sphere of our work under
modern conditions must perforce be specialized, but specialists need not live specialized
lives. I remember a little scholar from Scotland in my college at Oxford—mathematics
was his subject—who was asked by a fellow
undergraduate if he would come to a meeting
of the college debating society. He drew himself up with a look of grim and concentrated
resolution and replied, "No, I canna' come.
Ye see, I'm only mathematics". My friend,
you will observe, was not likely to fall a victim
to worldly distractions, but I wonder how far
he got in mathematics. Does an ill-balanced
life produce even the useful expert?

There is another balance which the university can help to strike. In the wise tradition of
this Foundation no one can embark on ad-
vanced studies before he has received the benefits of a liberal education. Such a provision
is more necessary as the sphere of knowledge

broadens and specialization narrows down
still further. When a scholar could approach
all natural science as the field of his endeavour, there was little danger of his vision
being narrowed, but now that science has sub-
divided itself almost infinitely, it is wise to
ask that the "contribution to original knowledge" upon which each doctor or master in
the making is working is, in some way however
remote, a contribution to actual life. Learning gains in value with one's ability to use it.
Osler inscribed the following passage from
Froude in a clinical note book which he had
prepared for his students:

> The knowledge which a man can use is the only
> real knowledge, the only knowledge which has life
> and growth in it and converts itself into practical
> power. The rest hangs like dust about the brain
> or dries like raindrops off the stones.

The highbrow who uses knowledge merely as
a mental decoration is not a university product. For the university exists not only to impart knowledge, but to develop in true proportion the qualities which can use it intelligently.

And in another sphere the university can
endow us with a sense of balance—in the professional school. Here a problem presents
itself which grows more difficult as the years

go on. With the increased demands made on
the candidates for a professional degree, and
the pressure of life in the professions themselves, how difficult it is for the undergraduate to co-operate in spirit with the wise provision, which this university was among the
first to institute, that none could receive a professional training who had not passed under
the influence of the liberal arts. But little
does this mean if the undergraduate regards
a few terms of history or the classics as a preliminary obstacle race to be got over before
the real contest begins. A profession can be
elevated into a vocation by the influence of a
mind which can see its relation to society. I
have always thought that, all things being
equal, I had far rather place myself under a
surgeon whose judgment had been trained,
whose sensibilities had been sharpened, by
some intellectual pastime unrelated to his
work, than under one whose science had remained stark and untempered by some knowledge of the humanities. I should have more
confidence in his judgment, in his sense of
proportion, in the balance of his view. If I
may quote Osler again:

> The practice of medicine is an art, not a trade;
> a calling, not a business; a calling in which your
> heart will be exercised equally with your head.

It is true of all professions that they need
something more even than intellectual equipment; they need the spiritual power with
which it is no less the privilege of the university to endow its sons.

How can such power be acquired? Not by
the mere mechanism of instruction. The most
magnificiently organized course labelled "humanities" will not produce the liberally-edu-
cated man. Under the stress of numbers we
are beginning to learn afresh what our fathers
knew well, that education must after all be derived from men as well as from books, and
perhaps more from men than from books. We
know that the elusive spark which comes from
the Gilmans, the Gildersleeves, and the Oslers
cannot come from the printed page, nor indeed
can it be transmitted to men in the mass, but
must be struck by the contact of mind with
mind. The process of education is indefinable,
and the highest gift of the university is equally
intangible, for it is a state of mind. Mental
qualities after all are independent of the
knowledge which the mind acquires. The
facts, the data of life, are but lifeless things
without purpose, courage, endurance, without
—to use an old-fashioned word—the quality
of wisdom. You are familiar with a well
known passage in De Quincey where he con-

trasts knowledge with power—the moral quality which gives reality to scientific truth:

> All the steps of knowledge—from first to last—
> carry you further on the same plane, but could
> never raise you one foot above your ancient level
> of earth; whereas the first step in power is a flight,
> is an ascending movement into another element
> where earth is forgotten.

Both knowledge and power are the gift of
the university and we must find the true balance between them.   Knowledge without the
moral power to use it has no reality.   On the
other hand, the noblest virtue, the finest idealism is unavailing, unarmed with science.   In
dealing with the façade of a building, architects use a formula which has always interested me.   They require a composition to show
a perfect balance between "the voids and
solids".   In other words, the masonry in its
mass and line must bear a happy relation to
the openings which pierce it.   Is it too remote,
too fanciful, to apply this principle to the
architecture of the mind which the university
does so much to form, and say that its structure too must show a due balance between
voids and solids, that the intellectual windows
through which come light and air, the intangible element, the idealism of life, must be truly

balanced with the concrete realities of the wall
—the masonry of knowledge?

I have mentioned some of those places in the
world of thought where proportion is hard-
est to preserve. Perhaps the problem that the
university can do most to help us solve, is to
strike a balance between the world of thought
and the world of action. The cynical critic
of modern society may say that before trying
to harmonize these two, we might do well to
prove that we have preserved some knowledge
of the first. But assuming both, we will be
happy if we can keep a just proportion between thinking and doing—between medita-
tion and movement. I was much struck in looking through a volume of essays written by your
first president to find that among the merits
of a university, he mentions "the cultivation
of a spirit of repose". Then follows a passage
written with feeling and conviction about "the
distractions of modern civilization" and "the
whirl of the nineteenth century" which make
a great university doubly valued and important as a "retreat for learned leisure". If
this was true in 1886 how much more must
we look now to the university as a refuge from
the turmoil which has been intensified in the
forty years since Dr. Gilman wrote these
words. For the university in the midst of the

clamour of modern life can remain serene and inviolate. But this is no easy task. The student inevitably reflects the age in confusing mere activity with accomplishment. There is a story of the great Master of Balliol, Dr. Jowett, who was told by a self-conscious and complacent undergraduate in confident anticipation of the Master's praise, that he was spending on an average ten hours a day reading for his examinations. "Indeed," was the reply, "and how many hours do you spend in thinking?" The rebuke may well apply to all sections of human life. Osler, if I may quote him once more, thought "the calm life necessary to continuous work for a high purpose".

Such tranquillity, of course, refers to personal equanimity which is superior to external distractions and clamours. But I do not think that we can quite overlook the relation of physical noise to spiritual calm. The religious society of which I believe your founder was a member, knew the power which is generated by silence. Silence, which in the old saying is golden, shines even more brightly, if less frequently, to-day. I wonder, Mr. President, whether science has ever come to grips with the question of noise in its relation to human efficiency and human happiness. If, as I sus-

pect, this is a field not yet systematically occupied, what a fine thing it would be for some
well-wisher of the human race to endow a
compaign of research into the elimination of
noise from the modern community. Think
what a co-ordination of effort it would entail
—a mobilization of physicists, psychologists,
psychiatrists, sociologists, municipal experts,
and at some moments I would add, criminolo-
gists, engaged in a crusade for the liberation
of human nerves from the bondage of din.

Well, sir, you will I hope be lenient towards
these random observations of a layman on
some aspects of a subject which at least he has
much at heart. Two things in conclusion I can
say with the fullest conviction of their truth.
First, I am happy to bring to you on your
fifty-second Commemoration Day the most
cordial greetings of the universities of Canada,
which are bound to you by so many personal
associations, but which beyond that are proud
to be allied with you in the performance of a
common task. Secondly, let me congratulate
you on this—that in all the contributions
which a university can make to its own members and the public at large, no institution of
higher learning in this wide country is render-
ing nobler service than this great university
in teaching youth to think; in extending and

diffusing human knowledge; and, to touch on
the central subject of these remarks, in helping all those in your midst to learn to lead a
balanced life.

CANADA'S NORTHERN FRONTIER

*Before the Bond Club of New
York, 2nd March, 1928*

Mr. President and Gentlemen:

When I was asked as to my subject I
thought it would not be inappropriate if a
Canadian guest, on this very pleasant occasion, should be permitted to make a few
remarks about Canada. You, of course, know
a good deal about our country. You are making a contribution here to its development
which is a significant factor in our progress.
You will, I am sure, not disagree with me when
I say that the progress is remarkable. During the last year the visitor to Canada has been
conscious of finding there an atmosphere of
reasoned optimism and quiet confidence which
is based on solid, indisputable fact. I have
been interested in looking over the reviews of
the past twelve months, which are part of the
harvest of that crop of annual general meetings which takes place each year in January
and February. I have been particularly interested in the reports of presidents of banks.
Bank presidents are not usually given to rash

statements. But nevertheless, I have found
that even in these conservative utterances
there is distinct evidence of the fact that in the
last year, in Canada, we have made a more
striking advance on a wider front, and with
what will be more permanent results, than in
any period of the same length in our history.

Last year we celebrated an anniversary
which meant a good deal to us in Canada, the
sixtieth anniversary of our confederation—
the diamond jubilee of our national unifica-
tion. We have therefore been thinking rather
more than we did before about our own past,
and consequently of our present and our
future too. It is sixty years since we became
a nation, but it is four centuries of course
since the first explorers sailed up the St.
Lawrence. What strikes one in looking over
the history of Canada is that we have been
exploring ever since that time. There is probably no country in the civilized world which
still has more exploration to do within its own
boundaries than our Dominion. It is surpris-
ing to find what a large area still has to be
accurately prospected and mapped. Now although the day of the voyageur and the early
settler is long past, I believe we have kept the
old spirit of exploration—the pioneer spirit
is still with us.

I was talking the other day with a friend of mine in Canada, who gave me an interesting example of how promise in our past has been fulfilled. When my friend was a boy he was told by his mother of a great series of plains west of Fort Garry (now Winnipeg), stretching eight hundred miles or so to the Rocky Mountains, inhabited by Indians, half-breeds and buffalo herds. He was told that this treeless land had been purchased from the Hudson's Bay Company for the stupendous sum of £300,000, and that the government of the day was very sharply criticized for the expenditure of such a huge sum. It was looked upon as rash extravagance. Fifty years and more after the event, during a short period a few years ago when we were passing through one of the temporary and quite natural periods of depression which are met with in a country where equipment and production must from time to time exceed the demand, my friend was asked to address a little gathering in a western city. He told of his recollection of the purchase of the Hudson's Bay lands, and then by way of contrast referred to something which he had just discovered in a publication of one of the western provinces, namely, the figure of its poultry production which, in that year, amounted to $2,000,000. In other words, the modest hen, in one province, produced in twelve months one third more in eggs and poultry than had been paid not only for that province, but for the three provinces—Manitoba, Saskatchewan, and Alberta, and part of British Columbia as well—only fifty years before. It was a reassuring thought.

The moments of economic depression which we have passed through now and then in Canada have always given us a very useful period of stock-taking, and have reminded us of the assets, always greater than we knew, which we possess. In the last twelve years, for instance, a period which covered the very difficult time of adjustment after the war, and the inflation which followed it, our bank deposits increased by $600,000,000, and still we were able to spend a similar amount in the purchase of motor cars.

May I tell you of another fact which is interesting? In 1915, when our first big war loan was under discussion, it was considered rather doubtful as to whether it would be wise to float an issue of such large proportions in Canada. At that time not a dollar of our federal government's indebtedness was held in Canada. The government of that day and succeeding governments acted with faith, with results which have been very striking, and now we find that eighty per cent. of the $2,400,000,000 of the existing federal debt is held within Canada by Canadians.

But what I wish to touch on particularly to-day is the progress which is being made in the development of our northern regions. We have always looked upon this area as unproductive, almost a wilderness. We have discovered however, within the last twenty-five or thirty years—and further discoveries are being made all the time—that this vast region contains treasure of which we never dreamed. Districts which seemed to present a problem now prove to be an asset. One of our great tasks, as you may know, is to widen the band of population which runs north of our border between east and west, and to fill the gaps in this ribbon of communities wherever the settlement is not continuous. This process is going on apace. For instance, it is now clear that one break in settlement, several hundreds of miles long, north of Lake Superior, will be productive of great wealth. What used to be regarded as a barrier between east and west is really coming to be a bridge. We used to say, in Canada, as you did in your country, "Go west, young man, go west". One of our most far-seeing public men has invented a new slogan, not to replace the other but to supplement it, which carries an appeal equally urgent—"Go north, young man, go north". There is now an advance on this northern line of ours in agriculture, in mining, in the development of water power and in the industries of the forest, which is almost unbelievable in its rapidity and extent.

In the natural wealth of Canada a very great factor is of course the stream of wheat which flows east from the prairies, and more recently to the west as well, in an increasing volume. It was in this sector of our northern battle front that the first push to the north took place. It took us some time to realize that, although our summer season was shorter, the days themselves are longer in the northern latitude; and that the long hours of sunshine with their effect on the ripening of grain compensate for the shorter season. To meet these conditions we have had to develop new types of grain. We are told by our experts that ninety per cent. of the wheat now grown in our west comes from a single seed which was produced after years of careful cross-breeding in Ottawa, twenty-five years ago. After further experiments we have produced a new kind of wheat—the Garnet—which took twelve years to develop. This type has recently been put to the test and is capable of shortening the ripening period by ten days. Its use will extend the margin of cultivation some one hundred and fifty miles further north. We can now, as a matter of fact, grow wheat profitably within four hundred miles of the Arctic Ocean. I heard not long ago of one actual achievement in wheat production, last year in Alberta, which sounds like a fairy tale. In one great wheat farm comprising a single field of thirteen hundred acres the average yield was fifty-seven and one-half bushels to the acre. This I believe constitutes a world record.

Perhaps the most spectacular sector in this northern frontier of ours is the one which you know a good deal about, here in New York, because you supply a considerable amount of its financial ammunition. I am referring to the sector occupied by the mines. An eminent Canadian business man a few weeks ago made a statement on our mining development which was most interesting. Quoting from government statistics he said that during eight of the first nine months last year, mining and its allied industries accounted for most of the freight on Canadian railways. We are therefore prepared to hear that 1927 marked a new high level in the output of our Canadian mines. The production for this year reached a figure of $241,000,000. A generation ago, in Canada, we used often to think of a mine as a hole in the ground of which frequently the principal output was in the form of alluring prospectuses. There may be still such holes in the ground, but I know of one which possesses eighty miles of underground passages, sixty-five miles of underground railway, and which will soon be crushing eight thousand tons of rock daily. One does not know how many potential developments of this magnitude there may not be in that great area known as the precambrian shield, which extends over five provinces of Canada, extending north as it moves to the west until it touches the Arctic Ocean. The soberest geologists kindle our imagination in describing the minerals which these regions bear. It is interesting to realize that the area which has produced minerals in Canada, up to date, covers less than one hundred square miles. The great area of potential mineral-bearing country covers two hundred and sixty thousand square miles. Experimental prospecting is of course being carried on on a large scale, but those of you who know the history of mining will remember that some of the richest mineral producing areas have been discovered by accident, for instance, the nickel deposits of Sudbury, con-

taining eighty-five per cent. of the world's
nickel, were found incidentally when the Canadian Pacific Railway was under construction
in the early 'eighties. Similarly the silver
mines of Cobalt were accidentally discovered
during the construction of a railway line
owned by the Government of Ontario.

In giving you these figures of our economic
development, I am painfully conscious of a
charge once made against a speaker (you will
suspect that this may be autobiographical)
that he was possessed of a statistical devil. I
promise you to keep statistics in check, but
let me just mention two more industrial activities in this northern region of ours. In
the development of water-power we now stand,
as far as the horse-power developed per
capita, second in the world. Norway is first.
We have generated five hundred horse-power
for every one thousand inhabitants, and this
process of development is proceeding with
amazing rapidity. When we realize that according to estimates about five-sixths of the
potential water-power we possess is still un-
harnessed, we will have some idea of what
lies ahead in this particular field in the near
future.

Closely allied to water-power is the pulp and
paper industry. In 1890 we exported prod-

ucts from paper mills to the aggregate amount of $120. In 1926 our exports under this head were well above $120,000,000, and now one-third of the world's newsprint comes from Canada. I have pleasure in pointing out to my newspaper friends that two-thirds of the paper used by the daily Press in this country now comes from across your northern border. As to the future, we are doing what we can to conserve our forests. I suppose the size of the Sunday editions of your newspapers can be said to have some bearing on the problem. The other day, when I heard of the installation of a machine, in one of our paper mills, which is capable of producing fifty acres of newsprint in an hour, I wondered whether you had decided to extend this weekly product beyond even its present proportions.

Transportation and communications represent an important element in warfare. They are no less important in the battle which we are waging against nature in our northern wilderness. Two new railways are now steadily nosing their way through the forests with the Hudson Bay as their ultimate objective. One of these in Ontario is being extended by the government of that province to James Bay, in order to tap the mines and forests of that area and carry settlement into this northern empire. The other—the Hudson Bay Railway—is being completed by the Dominion government and will shortly reach the old port of Churchill, in the Hudson Bay, which is now to be used again in the interests of modern commerce. This old-new route will bring the western provinces about a thousand miles nearer to Liverpool by sea. Over the doors of the Houses of Parliament at Ottawa are carved the words: "The wholesome sea is at her gates, her gates both east and west." We have found within the last few years that there is in this northern sea a new gateway— the Arctic Ocean itself—which we are learning to regard as within the bounds of the economic map of Canada.

We have still to find out accurately how many months the Hudson Straits are free from ice. In order that this information can be ascertained a patrol of airmen and mechanics and wireless operators was sent last autumn to the very tip of the Labrador peninsula and to the islands in the Straits, to reconnoitre the ice conditions and send in reports. This is a new use of the aeroplane in the interests of modern transportation. As a matter of fact, we have been constantly extending the usefulness of the airman in the last few years in the service of science. I

believe that about one-fourth of the pilots of
the Royal Air Force of Great Britain, during the war, were Canadians. Many of these
men are now employed by Canada in peaceful
exploits. The aeroplane provided the eyes of
the army during the war. It is no less the
eye for our new conquest of the north. Most
of the activities of our airmen are similar to
the work which your aviators are carrying on.
In a country with as much uninhabited terri-
tory as we have, and with our peculiar problems, it is natural that we should develop this
economic force to the limit of its capacity.
We use the aeroplane as you do in "timber
cruising", the detection and suppression of
forest fires, in assisting customs patrols, in-
specting fisheries and fighting wheat rust by
dusting the crops. We also use our airmen
to prospect possible water-power developments. We use them for topographical sur-
veying. Forty-five thousand miles of terri-
tory in Canada, I am told, were photographed
from the air and mapped last year, and now
we even use the aeroplane to assist the work
of the geologists and prospectors on foot in
their search for minerals, by revealing
through aerial photographs the location of
strata and the trend of mineral-bearing rock.
So now as a result of all this aerial activity,

the old *caches,* as the prospector called his
hidden supplies of food through the wilderness, are supplemented by no less necessary
caches of gasoline and oil, stored in recognized
places throughout our northern regions, which
tell their own story.

Well, gentlemen, I could tell you a great
deal more about this northern country of ours.
I could tell you of the work of policing this
area which is about the size of Europe, in
which our Royal Canadian Mounted Police
performs a service true to the traditions of
that famous force. In the annual report of
the Mounted Police, published not long ago,
underneath all the heavy restraint of official
language, there is enough romance for a library of novels. If one wonders whether the
pioneering instinct has left mankind, one can
be reassured in hearing that the Arctic patrols
of our Mounted Police are by no means regarded as unpopular duty, and that last year
there were over two thousand applicants to fill
just over one hundred vacancies in the force.

There are other things I should like to tell
you about in connection with the development
of this northern country but the time is too
short, gentlemen, to go into these by-paths. I
also want to show you that even a Canadian be-
guiled by such a hospitable atmosphere as this,

has some sense of restraint. Just one word more. In my remarks, I have made reference to what I have called our "northern frontier". As a matter of fact, I might have dropped the word "northern" because in the ordinary accepted sense of the word we have no southern "frontier". The term conjures up an atmosphere which we have not had on our border for over one hundred years. On each side of it is a vigorous nationality proud of and loyal to its own traditions. But we know that the international line is symbolized by the sincerest and fullest concord that can exist between two neighbouring nations. And in closing let me say what I know you have in your hearts as well as I have in mine. We hope that the knowledge and friendly understanding which exist between Canada and the United States, and between the United States and the Great Empire of which we in Canada are a part, may strengthen as the years go on.

THE UNIVERSITY
AND THE INTERNATIONAL MIND

*On the Occasion of the Sixtieth
Anniversary of the Founding of
the University of California,
Berkeley, 23rd March, 1928*

Mr. President, Ladies and Gentlemen:

There is something almost irresistible in the lure of California to those who dwell in the east and the north of this continent. I am glad that I have not attempted to resist the appeal, for as a visitor, I can see the reality behind it. And in this glorious spring of yours I appreciate the truth of the verses written by your own Bret Harte half a century ago, in which he says that California

> Breaks into blossom, flings the loveliest rose
> Ere the white crocus mounts Atlantic snows;
> And the example of her liberal creed
> Teaches the lesson that to-day we need.

You have a magnificent endowment of natural beauty, and the visitor is conscious that you are building cities which are worthy of their splendid setting. You have here also the ro-

mance of being a gateway between the ultimate west and the furthermost east. You
are thus a point of contact between the newest
world and the oldest, and therefore you are
strategically placed in time as well as in space.
But the gifts of nature and the works of man
are subordinate to man himself; the glory of
a community springs from the people who
compose it. You possess the enterprise and
imagination which will give reality to the
dreams of your founders. There is a passage
in Milton where he speaks (in the days before
language had become dully standardized) of
that happy state in which "the cheerfulness of
the people is so sprightly up as that it has not
only wherewith to guard its own person and
safety, but to spare, and bestow upon the solid-
est and sublimest points of controversy and
new invention". Here in a world of energy
and confidence you have this great Foundation
nobly dedicated to what Milton called "controversy and new invention"—intellectual activity and the advancement of learning—an
institution representing the finest expression
of the life of the community which it serves.
It is your own achievement. I was struck by
the passage in the inaugural address of your
first president, sixty years ago, when he said
in describing the plans for this university,

that it was to be "of the people and for the people . . . in the highest and noblest relations to their intellectual and moral well-being". This fine prophecy has been splendidly fulfilled. You celebrate to-day the completion of three score years of distinguished service. I congratulate you with all my heart and I am happy to bring to you the sincere and cordial greetings of the universities of Canada.

The universities of North America—in your country and in mine—have numerous ties. We have sent you many teachers and students as well. You have reciprocated in a degree greater than is perhaps realized. Although the foundations on each side of our mutual line are loyal to their own national traditions, they are ready to borrow ideas one from the other when it seems wise so to do. But beyond such personal and professional points of contact, important though they are, it seems to me that there is a still more significant bond of sympathy which unites such institutions the world over and which gives them an international as well as a national part to play. It is on this subject—the relations between universities and the affairs of nations—that I wish to address a few observations to you to-day.

I do so with the misgivings which are
proper, and also with the humility which is
becoming to a layman on academic ground.
If I talk of things whereof you know more
than I, I ask you to impute my failing to the
disarming grace of your hospitality. I often
feel that a diplomat rash enough to make a
public address must make a choice between
the Scylla of platitudes and the Charybdis of
indiscretions. Whichever I encounter I leave
it to you to judge, and to judge I hope with
Portia's comforting admonition in your
minds.

At the outset, I must confess, sir, that I am
painfully conscious of the depressing observation made, I think by La Bruyère, to the
effect that "everything has been said; and a
modern author comes too late by the seven
thousand years during which men have been
thinking". This probably is all too true.
However, if men have been thinking for seven
thousand years (this estimate must sometimes
seem to the wearied professor a gross exaggeration), let us be glad that universities have
existed for upwards of seven hundred years
to help them to think. The university has
been a growing power in the world since the
halls of Paris and Bologna commenced to be
a force in Europe, but the modern political

entity which we call a nation emerged from the
wreck of the mediaeval system which it destroyed only some three hundred years later.
The university thus has been thinking for a
much longer time than nations have been acting. But we need not think of the yardstick
of seniority in such a matter, for the importance of the place which universities occupy in
modern life itself, makes the question of their
contact with public affairs in all their aspects,
national or international, of a significance not
to be challenged.

Democracy has brought to the world gifts
past appraisal, and these we of the Anglo-
Saxon world are the first to realize. But democracy, so we must often tell its critics, is a
process of education as well as a form of government. It confers great privileges upon the
individual, but imposes the inevitable obligations as well. The first duty which it implies
is that which you understand so well in this
country—that of widespread education, its
highest aim being to produce the good citizen.
The meaning of citizenship has thus, through
the generations, been brought home with increasing clarity to those who possess it.
"Everyman", the type of universal human
being in the old morality play, has learned
that he is not alone in his pilgrimage, but that

he must share his rights and duties with his fellows in a great society. With the events of recent years his outlook has widened. We have learned that not only are the affairs of nations in the hands of Everyman, but that he is concerned no less with the relations between them. His ideas of foreign states, his suspicions of their motives, or his confidence in their goodwill—whatever his beliefs may be— these are upon what, in the last analysis, the actual relations between them will rest. Mr. Root has said:

> When foreign affairs were ruled by autocracies or oligarchies the danger of war was in sinister purpose. When foreign affairs are ruled by democracies the danger of war will be in mistaken beliefs.

Mistaken beliefs rest on inadequate knowledge, and lack of knowledge probably represents our major problem in the international world to-day. It is not hatred which divides nations but rather ignorance. When our ancestors were uncertain as to the characteristics of a country or the habits of its people, they wrote across the map without hesitation the agreeable legend, "Here are gryphons, hydras, and chimaeras dire". To-day the language may be different, but the ideas are not dissimilar, which some of us inscribe on the mental charts which we make of one another.

If there be danger of conflict, it will lie, as Mr. Root says, "in mistaken beliefs". Lord Bryce only a few years ago pointed out, speaking of the old world, that in no European country do the masses of the people know enough of their neighbours to enable them to form sound opinions in times of crisis. In these observations made, as it happens, by two men whose association in the sphere of international relations did so much to strengthen the understanding between our two nations here in North America, lies the essence of our problem.

When we look over the seven seas to-day, what is our view of the world of nations? We look to be sure upon a restless scene, but I wonder if the relations between peoples are more unfriendly than before. Is there less understanding between them than there was? Is it not fair to believe that the aftermath of the Great War has not created new problems so much as it has made us aware of old problems simply by revealing them in bolder relief? We view the scene often in false perspective. The news of conflict travels faster than that of concord. International crises are more easily described—make more thrilling reading than accounts of patient efforts to avert them and make them less likely. Yet during the last ten years or so there have been more minds bent on the task of maintaining peace than ever before. The goal of such effort has become no harder to attain. Events have taught us with graver insistence that it must be reached; but is there not in that a source of hope?

It should be easier to understand one another in this shrunken world. Science has done her best to bring us together. There never were so many points of physical contact between peoples: telegraphy, wireless, the broadcast radio, long-distance telephony, the aeroplane, and that dubious boon—television. All these have given us new international links, and yet it has been wisely suggested that mechanical means of communication may not have kept pace with the growing complexity of affairs the knowledge of which must be communicated. Mechanical points of contact, we may well believe, can be a peril in themselves for they can become friction points as well. I cannot help thinking of the homely illustration of the imperfect telephone connection which may leave the speakers at either end rather further apart than if the instrument had not been employed. It is of course clear that mechanical devices for international communication, like the mechanism of education, are not only useless but dangerous without wise control by intelligent minds. Few problems, after all, can be solved, few objects can be achieved, save through personal touch. International relationships are no less dependent on the human factor than are the processes of education.

But if science is helping to bring us closer together, human association, too, in its various forms is constantly providing new links between peoples. Not long ago I examined an authoritative publication which gives current data on the activities of voluntary bodies with an international scope and personnel. They seem to cover every aspect of human endeavour from religion and education and commerce and law, to hairdressing and clouds and eugenics and football, diamond-working and Esperanto. (There may be some significance in the existence in this formidable list of a body known as "The League for the Defence of Humanity".) Be that as it may, it is interesting to realize that of the four hundred international organizations in all, the oldest of which was founded in 1845, one hundred and eighty—nearly half—have been established in the few years since the commencement of the

Great War. Whatever may be one's view of these varied agencies, their existence is in itself evidence of the increased interest of the post-bellum world in its many problems.

But if the international picture is such a crowded canvas, where, you may ask, is there room within it for the university? What are its functions in such a sphere? How can it be of service? The question is interesting. Let us try to answer it. The university cannot act in any official capacity as has now and then been suggested. Dr. Lieber of Columbia University, in a letter to the Secretary of State of his day, once proposed the use of universities as official arbiters in international disputes. This was an intriguing suggestion but one to which I should be slow to subscribe. Not, I hope, because such an employment of universities might have a dislocating effect on the much abused profession of which I have become a member, or because (if it is not too flippant to suggest it) I have had enough experience of academic life to know that the collegiate cloister is often too much in need of diplomacy to have much to spare, but, more seriously, because I feel there is another role for the university in the international world more appropriate to its spirit. It is, I think, twofold. A modern university exists, we

know, to do two things—to think and to teach
—to advance the boundaries of human knowledge and to endow with such knowledge the
youth within its walls. In both these functions the university has become increasingly
conscious of the international world. It is
hard to estimate the contribution which it can
make wherever it exists to an understanding
of international problems. Your own well-
conceived "Institute of International Relations" is an example of the practical effective
interest which is being taken in this great subject. Through the many agencies through
which the work of a university is carried on—
the vast mechanism of lectures, libraries, researches, expeditions, conferences—an increased concern in the world at large is per-
ceptible. Universities everywhere are helping
the citizen to know how other peoples live,
what thoughts they think, what gods they
worship.

But perhaps in this sphere as well as in
others, as far as education is concerned (and
this is heresy I know), that knowledge which
is imparted informally, I was going to say unconsciously, is greater in its influence than the
instruction which is systematized and prescribed. The casual, informal half-hour with

professor or fellow-student may mean more
than either lecture or text-book. In the diffusion of knowledge of the international
world, the finest instrument which the world's
universities possess is provided by the movement between them of members of their own
personnel, the men and women who compose
them. If the knowledge and understanding
of peoples are best promoted by personal contact, the university of to-day is true to the
best in its distant past, when every centre of
learning attracted masters and students from
many lands. I cannot help thinking, here in
Berkeley, of one teacher, a member of my old
college at Oxford, Morse Stephens, who, as a
distinguished scholar of his own country, was
so generously adopted by yours. His own
library with its informal gatherings and the
vivid exchange of views carried on under his
influence, must have been in itself a little institute of international studies. I like to think
of those men like Stephens the world over, the
eminent scholars gone from your universities
to those of Great Britain and the continent
of Europe; others representing the older civilization here in the new, all engaged unconsciously through their students in spinning a
golden web of common understanding. Such

men see fundamental unities more easily than superficial differences, for to those who live on the high plane of scholarship the material walls between peoples present no barrier.

A scientific friend of mine, in referring to education in its international aspect, has coined a happy phrase—the "cross-fertilization of ideas". It would be interesting to know how many students to-day are engaged in such an operation. In botany, the object of cross-fertilization is to produce a finer flower. In the realm of the mind the corresponding process will yield no less happy an efflorescence of broadened view and deepened sympathy. There are now, I am told, between ten thousand and twenty thousand foreign students in this country profiting from your educational systems, and in turn telling you of the problems and aspirations which they have left at home and to which most of them will in time return. An increasing number now come and go under permanent foundations. I am always stirred in reading the annual list of those chosen to enjoy the benefits of such great systems of fellowships in the United States as those bearing the names of Rockefeller and Guggenheim, which send each year a corps of selected scholars from your institutions to study in the universities of the world and in all fields of learning. There is no country with so fine a tradition in the use of private wealth for public purposes as yours, and this munificence, never so generous as when directed to education, has set up foundations too numerous to mention, carrying students to other lands and bringing men and women to study here. Such an interchanging pilgrimage of study can bridge a veritable ocean of misunderstanding.

Next year will complete the first quarter century of what is perhaps still the greatest adventure in the realm of international education—the foundation which bears the name of Cecil Rhodes. The romance of the founder's life we know: exiled to South Africa a hopeless invalid, snatching an Oxford education under grave handicaps and, in the few and unexpected years given him, erecting a new empire in the African wilderness. But the man who is buried in the great stark tomb in the Matopo Hills—on the site which he himself had called in unconscious prophecy "The World's View"—will be remembered not so much for his achievement as for the greatness of the conception interwoven in his famous will. Kipling says what posterity will think of him:

So huge the all-mastering thought that drove—
    So brief the term allowed—
Nations, not words, he linked to prove
    His faith before the crowd.

He believed with all his heart, as do so many of us, that the peace and welfare of the world rest on the unity of the English-speaking peoples, and he believed too that such unity, which must be a unity of the spirit, could be achieved only by spiritual processes. "Educational bonds are the strongest", he said. Rhodes used the words meaning the bonds of sympathy and understanding which he believed his foundation would serve to strengthen, but it was to do so, he wisely hoped, (to quote his words) "without drawing them [the scholars] or their sympathies from the land of their adoption or birth". So as a result of what this practical dreamer did, two hundred youths personifying the energy and keenness and versatility of the new world are now constantly in touch with those who represent the best tradition of the old—creating good feeling and good fellowship and exchanging or sharing ideas.

There are many ideas to be shared. The student from America who enters Oxford or Cambridge—and there are, I am told, as many

from this country at the latter university as
there were Rhodes Scholars at Oxford when
the foundation was established—and the increasing number of British students who come
to study here, will discover that the universities on both sides of the water are, in many
respects, strikingly alike, and equally different
from those on the continent of Europe. They
will find in both much the same conception of
a liberal education. They will find the same
Anglo-Saxon tradition of games. They will
find moral as well as mental values entering
into the plan of higher education. Under-
graduates, throughout the English-speaking
world, as a matter of fact are united in a
vigorous, perhaps slightly overstated, distrust
of the intellectual type. There are, on the
other hand, real differences between the universities on both sides of the Atlantic. The
English college, true to English characteristics, is dominated by a solicitude for the individual and its system is mainly directed to
his development. Universities on this continent have risen superbly to the great task of
teaching the maximum number, and through
their splendid organization and equipment
have carried education to the community as a
whole. But however like or unlike may be the
methods or the tasks of universities, the

scholar who moves from one country to the other, no matter whence he comes or where he studies, will find his loyalty to the best of what is in his own system strengthened and not weakened by seeing it for a time in the perspective of distance. If he is sound at heart, his understanding of other points of view will be deepened without the need of accepting the points of view of others, or without the impairment of his allegiance to what is his own. No real personality has anything to fear from the adoption from any source of what is worth adopting.

One asks, are the Rhodes Scholarships a success? But is there any question? One cannot appraise any educational scheme in terms of figures and percentages. The success of the Rhodes plan rests on a few hundred men selected for their promise of good citizenship. Their services to their own country on their return may be in the public eye or not—it is none the less real. But if one asks for tangible proof—if one seeks as it were a sign —it is not wanting. In my own country you can find Rhodes Scholars—the oldest just reaching the prime of life—in positions of leadership throughout the Dominion. Two are members of Parliament. As for your own country, you have but to consult the records.

Distinguished achievement and high office, as
well as the silent influence of unobtrusive service, belong to these venturers in education.
It is no small privilege for the ancient university which for a season had these men
under her spell that she, through her service
on their behalf, can make some contribution
to your life.

One characteristic of the university everywhere, and an increasing one, is to carry on
its work in terms of not one but many nations.
But if universities can serve the cause of international understanding as a sort of by-
product of their activities, why not, it may be
asked, create international universities where
the study of such problems would be the major
object and in which the personnel would be
selected from the world at large? Such, in my
belief, is not the way. The university can best
play its part in international concord when it
has itself a national character and reflects
honestly and with clarity the finest characteristics of the nation which it serves. Colourless cosmopolitanism has no place in the academic world—nor indeed elsewhere. When I
visit a university in another land, my first desire is to see in it the ideas and activities of
its own country expressed in their highest
form; and in order to reflect the atmosphere of

its own community for the benefit of others, the university must first of all be a homogenous product itself. The role of interpreter cannot be approached through some composite language which no one speaks. All useful functions are best performed by nations, universities, or human beings possessed of a strong personality. The university should remain true to its own traditions and without evasion or overstatement interpret them wisely to others.

As with the university so with the nation itself. The counsel of Polonius, and its conclusion too, belong no less to the state than to the individual:

To thine own self be true;

· · · · · · · · · · · · · ·

Thou canst not then be false to any man.

The nation, self-conscious and self-respecting, is not only compatible with world concord but even underlies it. Nationality, far from being an obstacle to world peace is, rightly understood, the very pillar on which it must rest. *Ut pro patria, ita pro orbis concordia* runs a Latin phrase. The nation is, as someone has said, a link in the chain between the individual and humanity. The wise educationist will so regard it. I cannot sympathize with the

efforts, however well intentioned, to de-
nationalize education. How difficult to induce
boys and girls to cheer for an abstract idea
such as universal brotherhood, but how natural
to ask them to show some enthusiasm for the
contribution which their country may be making to the universal brotherhood.

But how to relate the claims of nationality
with our obligations to humanity—how to reconcile the full freedom of the part with the
concord of the whole? This will require the
dispassionate effort of informed and instructed minds—minds equipped with knowledge
of the world but endowed with something
more. I have spoken of the knowledge which
the university exists to impart. It can give
us something beyond even knowledge—the
state of mind which knows how to use knowledge; which discerns principles, understands
human nature, is not only "subtle enough to
deal with things" but "simple enough to deal
with men", is tolerant of others, welcoming
and not despising differences. Tolerance and
understanding are almost a test of civilization itself, and such qualities are in the very
spirit of a university. They belong to it no
less than the formulae of the laboratory.
Understanding is needed, as well as knowledge; feeling, as well as thinking. It was

Churton Collins who said that "half our mis-
takes in life arise from feeling where we ought
to think and thinking where we ought to feel".
Great problems must be approached with a
combination of both faculties. So with our
problem to-day. The world needs knowledge
and wisdom—probably more of wisdom than
of knowledge. It is rarer and more precious
and more lasting. "Knowledge comes but wisdom lingers" sang Tennyson. If we look to
the university as an interpreter, the spiritual
language, the language of the mind which it
speaks, generous, sympathetic, and understanding, will do more for us than even the
facts and data of life, essential though they
are. It is important to know one's neighbours; it is more important to understand
them—and the elements of life which are most
significant are those which cannot be weighed
and measured. Even the most practical and
the most realistic of modern statesmen was
compelled to admit the significance of what he
called the "imponderables".

The world has long cherished the ideal of
an international order in which nations will
express their traditions and their aspirations
no less strongly than they do now, but in terms
of the arts of peace; in which those differences
which must occur will be settled no longer by

the cruel fantastic method of the sword; where
the nations will be under the jurisdiction not
of some super-state, but of something far more
compelling, a conception of order and law—
not on paper only—but in the minds of men.
When such an idea prevails then the earth will
be released from the shadow of war. Lord
Cecil has said that civilization is after all only
"man's progress from isolation to co-operation". We have gone further on the road than
we know. We look to the university wherever
it exists to help us on the journey, to instruct
us, to give us the knowledge on which to base
judgments, and to endow us with the wisdom
with which our judgments must be formed.

We look to the university and to its sons
and daughters as well. The students of to-
day are fortunate, and despite what may now
and then be said, I believe that the young men
and women who throng our universities are
not ungrateful for the privileges which an
older generation has lavished upon them.
They can realize, also, the privilege which
comes with the gift of education—that of playing a worthy part in the affairs of their time.
No age has offered its youth greater opportunities for high courage, generous ardours
and splendid adventure. The world lies glori-
ously plastic for their shaping. If I mistake

not, our grandsons will be able to say of our
time what Wordsworth said of another:

> Bliss was it in that dawn to be alive;
> But to be young was very heaven.

One word more. It is not new, this idea
which I wish to leave with you. You have
heard it before, but it is the most important
idea in human affairs to-day. In this world
of swift change and mingled discord and hope-
fulness, we of the English-speaking nations
must maintain that harmony which is true
both to our own past and to the world's future.
Where differences exist, let us face them and
respect them. Where common ideals prevail,
let us cherish them. Your great Republic and
the Dominion on your north, and the ancient
Empire to which we in Canada so happily
belong, are united above all in a common love
of peace. Let us stand together in mutual confidence, and let us hope for a hastening of the
day when men the world over will be able and
willing "to see life steadily and see it whole".

THE BASIS OF PEACE

On the Occasion of the Celebration of the Centenary of the American Peace Society, Cleveland, Ohio, 9th May, 1928

My first duty this evening, Mr. Chairman, and a most agreeable one, is to convey to the president and members of the American Peace Society the most cordial congratulations of my country on the completion of one hundred years of distinguished service in the cause of international understanding. As the representative of His Majesty's Government in Canada, and on behalf of the Canadian public as well, I am happy to convey to you, sir, our warmest felicitations on a century of usefulness, together with our best wishes for success in the second hundred years of effort of which this occasion may be regarded as the inauguration.

The American Peace Society is one of the oldest bodies in the world devoted to the cause of peace. No organization existing for this purpose was, I believe, ever established until after the Napoleonic wars, and then several came into being on both sides of the Atlantic. I think the oldest survivor of these is the London Peace Society which was founded in 1816. The American Peace Society came soon after. One realizes what a pioneer in this great field of endeavour it was, in discovering that as early as in 1829, the society offered a prize of thirty dollars for the best "Dissertation on the subject of a Congress of Nations". The committee of the day, so I am told, showed a commendable spirit of thrift in proposing to the successful candidate, as his reward, the choice of honorary membership in the society, or the award of a gold medal, or, lastly, the money itself. The fact that only two essays were submitted perhaps suggests the magnitude of the task assumed by the society in interesting the public of the day in the subject of international conciliation. Be that as it may, the interest in the problems of world peace has grown past computation in the generations covered by the history of this society, and its own work has played no small part in this development in the wide community which it serves.

The years from 1828 to 1928 cover a period of great significance in the history of all the nations which are represented here this evening. The first of those years, Mr. Chairman,

found your own Republic a united nation of
only some two score years standing, in population but one-tenth of what you possess to-day.
Your area was far less than it now is. Actual
settlement, or indeed man's imagination, had
by that time hardly bridged the Mississippi
River. The Latin peoples of South and Central America, who have sent distinguished representatives to these meetings, had in 1828 (as
far as the mainland is concerned) only just
acquired their own sovereignty and the control of their own destiny in the world of nations. There is no part of the Americas where
a greater change has taken place in these hundred years, than in the country which I am
privileged to represent. Like you we have
grown in stature. One hundred years ago
Canada—(or what later was to become Canada)—was composed of a few hundred thous-
and people, some in Quebec, fewer in the upper province, and the remainder in scattered
settlements far away by the sea. To the west
and to the north lay an illimitable wilderness.
The northern Pacific coast to us as to you was
a no-man's land. In the generations that followed we discovered, in the revelations of
wealth in our vast domain, that there is no
such thing as wilderness. The term may apply to scenery but it has no economic mean-

ing. So we have found through the riches
hidden in lands which for so long we thought
barren.

And as we have grown in stature we have
changed no less in other ways. In 1828, our
form of government resembled that from
which you emerged in the previous century.
Before the hundred years had passed we had
acquired a freedom in control of our affairs
no less than yours to-day. This change represented no transfer of sovereignty, for we live
under the same Crown. But little alteration
in outward form has taken place; we have
preserved the old traditions wherever possible.
But the year 1828 comes close to the beginning
of that long debate which turned the old colonial system into the modern British Empire,
and as a result of which century-long discussion, Canada together with the newer Dominions acquired the rights and responsibilities
of a sovereign state within the British Empire's broad and generous bounds.

You have called this Neighbour's Day.
Perhaps I may be permitted in default of a
worthier representative to say a word not only
for Canada but also for those scattered British
communities who are kinsmen of ours, and are
happy to live as are we in Canada, under the
Union Jack, and subjects of the same king, but

like ourselves are friendly neighbours of yours and the other nations of the Americas. A scattered group they are. They include the ancient colony of Newfoundland, autonomous in all respects, Bermuda, possessing the most ancient legislature in the British Empire, except the mother of Parliaments itself, and so on—colonies in every stage of self-government, down to the islands in the Caribbean and settlements on the mainland with the simplest form of administration. The British Empire presents a multi-coloured pattern, so varied are its forms of government, so diversified its communities. But we have learned in this Commonwealth of ours that diversity is the very mother of unity itself.

So here we meet, Republic and Empire, nations and colonies, islands and continents, old and new. Differences there are in plenty in the Americas, but we can nevertheless meet as neighbours, with all that old word means. I think it was Mr. John Hay who once said in a light-hearted mood: "Love your neighbours, but be careful of your neighbourhood." We have abundant reason to be thankful for our neighbourhood in the western hemisphere. Not only for all that nature has given us, but for the traditions of peaceful relations which we have been fortunate enough to establish here ourselves. Canada is unique among the nations in having only one near neighbour, and the concord between these neighbours has become almost proverbial. It commenced long ago.

At a gathering such as this it will not be inappropriate to point out that North America provides one of the earliest instances of the principle of international arbitration being embodied in a convention between two states. Students of history will not need to be reminded that, in the famous "Treaty of Amity, Commerce and Navigation" as it was called, drawn up by John Jay and Lord Grenville, in 1794, it was provided that an important question relating to the boundary between New Brunswick and the United States should be referred to arbitration. Four years later the arbitration had successfully taken place. We can also boast of an early successful achievement in disarmament in that exchange of Notes in 1817, known as the Rush-Bagot Agreement, which placed a limitation on the naval forces to be maintained on the great lakes.

It is easy, however, for us here in North America, remote from the friction points of history, to forget the legacy of immemorial strife under which the statesmen of Europe

labour. The wonder is often not that the recovery of the older continent from past events
is slow, but rather that those who guide its
destinies have been able to do so much in
recent years towards the establishment of a
lasting peace. But fortunate as we have been,
here in North America, in the inheritance of
a vast continent with natural wealth, and room
beyond our needs, and no evil inheritance of
prejudice, we may point with some pride to
a tradition of tolerance and common sense in
our dealings with each other. It is true that
in our enthusiastic moments we refer to our
peaceful border in unrestrained imagery, but
underneath our rhetoric there is solid fact.
When anyone asks what actual steps we have
taken to give this boundary the character of
which we boast, we can point to real machinery
which marks the nature of our relations in
order to answer, if need be, the charge that we
are idly generalizing.

The sceptic, however, will direct our gaze
elsewhere, and after a survey of the world
will ask us to listen to those rumours of war
to which, as has been pointed out, we seem to
attach more "news value" than to forecasts
of peace. He will say, "Why hope for peace
when a century of effort to bring harmony into
the world served as a prelude to the greatest

war in history?" But sceptics are notoriously
myopic. They fail to see that more human
beings are now bent on preventing wars, more
people are thinking in terms of peace, and that
governments are directing their energies to
this end as they never have done in the past.
Do we hear more of war? The fact is that we
are more conscious of the cruelty and futility
of war than ever before and therein lies the
hope, for the consciousness of a disease is the
first step towards its diagnosis and cure.

But the sceptic is persistent. "Why found
societies just to encourage peace? Why talk
about it?" he will ask, "Why not take some
action?" Well, ladies and gentlemen, it seems
to me that a most important thing is just to go
on talking about it! There is supposed to be
a distinction between words and deeds. A
word is really a deed, if it expresses an idea.
For ideas are the most practical, even the most
explosive things in the world. The ideas, the
knowledge and the perceptions which bodies
like this distinguished society are now spreading all over the world, must sooner or later
prove a match for the forces with which they
have to cope. The fact that there are more
people now talking about peace and thinking
about peace, and bent on peace, is one of the
most reassuring things to be found to-day.

Idealism of all kinds, of course, encounters many perils. Not the least of these is that to be met in high mental altitudes, the lofty atmosphere where the oxygen of reality is rarest. To keep in touch with cold, hard, concrete facts and yet not to lose the vision all the while; to have a grasp of actualities and yet to keep the ideal—that is a difficult balance to preserve. The peace movement must be one of the head as well as of the heart—sound thinking must accompany goodwill. I wonder if we are sufficiently careful of the distinction between education and propaganda. One seeks the light, the other prefers the half-light which can only distort. One is concerned with truth, the other satisfied with half-truth. One dodges no fact however awkward, the other evades what is embarrassing and only builds a structure without a true foundation. In the Anglo-Saxon world we have injured many a good cause by well-intentioned movements which have refused to meet brute facts. Time was when the movement for peace was associated in our minds often with the sentimental and the unreal—deliberate unpreparedness, vapid cosmopolitanism. It suggested a vague movement upward but without earthly direction. To-day the cause is represented by constructive methods, sternly practical ends. Its ideals take full cognizance of human nature. The peace movement of to-day has wisely brought science to its aid; the knowledge of the forces that make for war are allied with the will to overcome them. It is not propagandist but educational in the finest sense of the word.

I do not suppose that the object of the millions of human beings who are groping towards universal peace can be better expressed than in the constitution of your society, where it is said that its purpose is to "promote permanent international peace through justice". In other words, the objective is the rule of law in the world of nations. Just as individuals in the dark ages found themselves happier in the new conception of the "king's peace", when order first dawned in those rudimentary kingdoms, so will the sixty odd collective personalities which we call sovereign states, be the richer and the happier for the prevalence of a greater conception of peace.

The domestic peace, in modern democracies, reposes ultimately on the maintenance by the community as a whole of certain rules for the control of their conduct. Underlying it all and making it possible is a collective state of mind. Is the problem of peace among nations at all different in essentials? Lawyers talk of sovereignty, diplomats of sanctions, but more important than either is that attitude of mind among peoples which will make possible the acceptance of reasonable rules to govern their relations and settle their differences. Therefore, underlying international law and diplomacy, and even statesmanship, it seems to me, is the world-wide education in international affairs without which none of these can function. For this reason we must be grateful for those who are responsible for the success of this venerable society, and all other agencies everywhere existing for the diffusion of knowledge as well as the promotion of goodwill between peoples. That way lies universal peace.

Knowledge we must have. We must know one another. From better knowledge there will flow mutual understanding and forbearance and confidence. In such an atmosphere the impossible can be accomplished. The way may be long. The pace cannot be forced. Disarmament, mental as well as physical, must needs be gradual, but the progress surely can be steady and real and increasing. The goal will be achieved, for the idea for which this society and the growing army of like-minded people stands, the world over, is imperishable. Like truth itself, it will prevail.

GOOD NEIGHBOURHOOD

"... and thereby to promote a disposition favourable to friendship and good neighbourhood . . ."—JAY'S TREATY, 1794.

At a Dinner given by the Pilgrims of the United States in Honour of the Canadian Minister and a Group of Gentlemen Representative of the Public Life of Canada, New York, 10th December, 1928

Mr. Chairman and Gentlemen:

May I say in the first place how deeply and gratefully conscious we from Canada are to-night that all of us in this room are one in our anxiety over the bulletins from London. We are earnestly hoping and praying for more reassuring news of His Majesty the King. Let me tell you how deeply we appreciate the sympathetic understanding which is visible everywhere in this great country, and your willingness to share in our hopes and prayers for His Majesty's recovery.

I wish to join, sir, with my fellow Canadians

175

here in expressing my heartfelt gratitude for the graceful tribute which has been paid to our country this evening by the eminent society of which we are so glad to be the guests. For a quarter of a century the Pilgrims of the United States have been a distinguished body standing for a noble ideal—friendship between this great Republic and the Empire to which we, in Canada, are so proud to belong. This fine ideal, so vital to the well-being of the world at large, has been eloquently and ably expressed at the many gatherings held under the society's auspices. But it has been a matter of practice as well as of precept. For occasions like this—when under your generous hospitality citizens of different countries are brought into the comradeship of a common board—such occasions lie at the very roots of international good-fellowship.

I feel, sir, that I must confess to certain grave personal misgivings as to my own role this evening. When our distinguished chairman first made the suggestion to me of to-night's dinner I told him that as a Canadian I was touched by his generous proposal. I stipulated, however, as I thought (and this was in your interests as well as mine) that whatever part he desired the Canadian representative at Washington to play in the evening should be reduced to negligible, even inaudible proportions. I feel the voice of this official is already heard too frequently in the hospitable land to which he is accredited. I may say, gentlemen, that in my innocence I thought that my function was to say a word of introduction on behalf of my good friends from Canada and to make way for them. I conceived my part to-night to be like that played by a silent figure which for many years belonged to a great Chicago packing-house. He was a very humble steer, an under-nourished beast—too thin himself to be productive of much meat (here I feel the similarity between us is peculiarly strong). His duties lay on the runway leading to the place of execution, and consisted in leading his stouter and more worthy fellows through the fatal door. But he was possessed of such modesty that he himself always stepped to one side at the right moment, leaving the others in a position where, let us say, the community was able to benefit from what they had to give. Now Dr. Butler, with a combination of executive efficiency and academic shrewdness, has usurped my role and, alas! I find myself on the runway with no chance of escape.

It is now nearly two years, gentlemen, since you were the friendly hosts of a newly arrived,

very inexperienced Canadian diplomat who
made his first public appearance under your
generous hospitality. I shall never forget the
warmth of your welcome. And the months
which followed have shown that that welcome
was a true forecast of the reception which
Canada's representative was to receive everywhere he went in your great country. My wife
and I have had the pleasure of visiting many
parts of this vast Republic—I may say that
it is our ambition to see something of every
one of the forty-eight states before we leave
you—and wherever we have gone we have been
touched by the prevailing cordiality and
friendliness towards your northern neighbour.
This feeling makes my work at Washington
and my relationships both official and personal
everywhere a source of genuine pleasure.

Diplomacy between our two countries here
in North America has after all a simple technique, or perhaps it would be true to say
no technique at all. In all our many dealings
with each other, each nation has learned to
assume on the part of its corporate neighbour
just the same common sense and spirit of give
and take that it expects of its own citizens.
Our mutual frontier offers proof enough of
this. This famous boundary of ours has never
lacked ample public references to its unique

characteristics. But after all it is natural and proper that we should regard it as genuinely expressive of what international relationships should be. The other day I came across a forgotten treaty of 1850 between Great Britain and the United States which illustrates the atmosphere. Your government desired to build a lighthouse at the upper end of the Niagara River. It was found that the selected spot was British soil. But that offered no obstacle, for His Majesty's government ceded you the island where, to this day, this American lighthouse may be seen generously shedding its light to all ships that pass, securely based upon British rock. You promised in the treaty not to fortify the lighthouse, and as far as I can see from a passing train, sir, no guns have as yet appeared!

As it happens, there frequently pass over my desk communications dealing with the movement of troops up to the border and across it. How warlike it sounds! But you may rest content in knowing that these cases of military mobilization represent only acts of courtesy, the expression of the very good feeling which armies elsewhere too often serve to threaten. So, now and then we receive a squadron of your airmen on a complimentary flight to Canada, or one of our Highland regiments visits you on a corresponding mission of friendship.

A few months ago I heard Mr. Hughes observe in referring to our relations here in North America that, "We have nothing to fight about and much to discuss". That we have nothing to fight about there is no question, but two years at the Canadian Legation in Washington have convinced me that we have plenty to discuss. And that is natural. Our boundary is crossed each year by millions of human beings and hundreds of millions' worth of commodities. Such a vast traffic creates its own problems. If our frontier is made safe by modern common sense, it is made very complicated by modern science. The aeroplane, the hydraulic turbine, the wireless transmitter, the gasoline motor, the irrigation ditch, the submarine cable are a few of the inventions each of which has added its quota of problems to the boundaries of to-day. And nature, too, plays a large part in modern diplomacy, for we have found that even the fowls of the air and the fish in the sea, and the denizens of the insect world must now and then be the subject of international agreement. There are fifty-eight treaties and conventions at present in force which govern our relations under many heads. Nine permanent international bodies are charged with the supervision of various international interests. If this mechanism did not operate so smoothly and efficiently the public would be more aware of its existence. The questions may be many and varied but they are settled as they arise; when possible, before they arise. For such is the function of diplomacy. Like modern medicine it must concentrate on prevention rather than cure.

It cannot be said that the friendship which flows between us is due to any lack of individuality on the part of the two neighbours. There are vigorous national personalities on both sides of the line. They have a cousinly resemblance which is not incompatible with the special characteristics which each possesses along with the differences in background, in size and in age which mark us. In age your northern neighbour can be said to be both old and young. We have inherited an ancient tradition, but as a nation Canada's full responsibilities were first assumed in the four desperate years which followed the August of 1914. During the decade which has followed the war, Canada has been glad to play her part in the great movements which have peace as their end. In this connection may I say that we are proud of being among the first to sign the great Pact of Paris of August last, which was brought into being by your government.

But we cannot think only of the formal acts which have peace as their objective. These have their importance not to be measured, but peace, of course, is more than action, it is an idea that must precede and stimulate action. As wise men have said, peace is nothing more than education. It is, after all, simply education in the art of getting on together. It may be on a big scale or on a small scale. Whether it is an accommodation between the rivalries of two villages or the conflicting aspirations of two nations the principle is just the same. Practice on a small scale may be an education for the larger. Peoples with an Anglo-Saxon tradition should know how to harmonize their differences, because the race has had a thousand years of practice within itself. English history for centuries marked the gradual accommodation of national unity with that healthy, stubborn passion for local freedom which is the greatest gift that England has given to the world. It is the spirit which lies at the foundation of this country; and also of every country which flies the British flag. Each community in the Anglo-Saxon world has had to reconcile the innate sense of local rights with the unity and safety of the whole. Deep down in the Anglo-Saxon nature the world over is enshrined the belief that the toleration of differences is the measure of civilization.

Canada can be said to be interested in peace and harmony in three spheres. First, like most nations, we have had the education of our own experience. The foundation of our domestic harmony in Canada was laid generations ago. Scattered communities had to be unified without jeopardy to their historic privileges. We learned, as you did here, how this could be done under a federal system. We saw how the various units of population which now make up the Dominion could live together with individual freedom, and yet with joint co-operation within the boundaries of a single state. Two of these communities possess different traditions, faiths and languages. They live side by side in amity. The consequence is that Canada enjoys the gifts of two great races instead of one, and in an age when standardization is one of the deadly foes of society we have a diversity which is a blessing in itself. We are grateful for the rich colour and the beauty which are given us by the ancient province on the St. Lawrence and for the great contribution which its citizens are making to the life of the Dominion as a whole.

I have mentioned our domestic harmony. There is a second harmony in a wider field which we have taken our share in bringing about. Not a conciliation within ourselves this time but within the family—the reconciliation between two principles in the great empire of which we are a member. Again we see the unity of the whole reconciled with the full development of the parts which compose it. On Canadian soil many of the great issues in the history of the British Commonwealth were worked out. As we assumed, at each step, a fuller measure of autonomy, our loyalty to the larger unity and our devotion to the Throne which symbolizes it were sensibly deepened and quickened. It sounds like a paradox. But paradoxes are often the truest things in life. In the various diverse units which make up our Commonwealth one can find the toleration of differences practised on the greatest scale yet seen in the world. Perhaps we should say not the toleration of differences but rather the consecration of differences, so full in this great fabric is the allowance for local feeling and local pride. I mention our Empire here to-night, conscious, as I have learned by experience, how many sincere well-wishers it has here in this country.

I have just mentioned two of the harmonies

with which we Canadians are concerned—one amongst ourselves, the other in the family circle. Let me return to the third, for I have touched on it already. In an ancient treaty between the American and British peoples its major purpose is declared to be "to promote a disposition favourable to friendship and good neighbourhood". The pious aspirations in the preambles of treaties have often remained nothing more. In this case it has been different. In the century and a third since this fine phrase was written, "friendship and good neighbourhood" in North America have become very real. We do not talk much about the amity between us—we practise it. It does not exist, as I have said, because either of the North American neighbours lacks individuality. It is rather, I believe, because each has it. In fact I would suggest that one of the reasons for mutual respect between nations anywhere is their own self-respect. Our own self-confidence in Canada has been greatly quickened with the sense of nationality which has grown over the last few generations. It is also as true to say that as our confidence in our own future has deepened over the years, our relations with our neighbour have steadily improved. On the other hand we in Canada recognize and appreciate your generous acclaim of our national aspirations.

We agree on fundamentals, and yet we have learned to recognize our differences. One is as important as the other. Amongst the American and British peoples the world over there is a great heritage of common traditions, such as our literature, law and our historical background; but the strongest common characteristic of the Anglo-Saxon, let us never forget, is his incorrigible individualism. It is that which is in the warp and woof of every Anglo-Saxon community. There is no virtue in uniformity of outlook—there is always a danger in exaggerating similarity. How foolish it is to assume, for instance, that civilization in this country is simply English civilization moved overseas, instead of being something increasingly different and new. The recognition of differences, after all, is the beginning of understanding. Understanding means mutual confidence. And that is the only principle on which international security can be based.

Mutual confidence is the principle of our own common boundary. How have we achieved it? There is no secret formula but there is one reason, a simple, practical, even obvious reason for our "friendship and good neighbourhood". To the old adage "Know thyself" we have added another, "Know thy neighbour". We know one another here in North America and from that mutual knowledge flows all the mutual confidence, all the understanding underlying our relations. We must, of course, have knowledge, not half knowledge. The latter leads to a sort of twilight of misunderstanding, but full knowledge —personal knowledge—is a sun which can melt even prejudice. The American and British peoples have no excuse for not knowing one another. Most of them can speak the same tongue, and if distance between some of our respective peoples be thought a barrier to understanding we live, after all, in an age which is defying distance. But even a single language will not help us if we never meet except through telegrams. At long range a common tongue can almost be a common peril. There is no scientific substitute for the conversations, the visits, the personal meetings on which human relations have always rested. I hope it is not too frivolous to suggest that if one month a year by universal consent was declared a close season for all cabinets, councils and legislatures, and that for this period the responsible statesmen were induced to forgather and take up fishing rod and golf club,

with not a whisper of "shop", the harmony
of the world might be enhanced. It would
most certainly not be impaired.

There have never been so many human
beings thinking of peace and working for
peace as now. That in itself should be our encouragement. An increasing number of men
and women of all countries are engaged, as
individuals or in corporate bodies like this,
in an endeavour to bridge the "unplumb'd,
salt, estranging sea" of ignorance and prejudice. The name of your great society, the
Pilgrims, suggests the nature of the movement
the world over. No great faith has been without its pilgrimage. The objective may have
been Benares, or Jerusalem, or Mecca, or
Rome, or your own Plymouth Rock, but in
every case there was a goal, a movement towards it, and comradeship by the way. The
goal of which all of us here to-night are thinking is the understanding between nations. It
has no place on a terrestrial map, but it is none
the less real, for it is a state of mind which can
see life in its true proportions and can banish
the misunderstanding between peoples.

You may remember some lines in the play
by John Drinkwater which will stand as an
English tribute to the great figure of Lincoln
which you have given to the world. The

author, after touching upon the tranquillizing effect of the beauties of the country-side on a war-torn community, says:

> Does not every threshold seek
> Meadows and the flight of birds
> For compassion still?
>
> . . . .
>
> Are we pilgrims yet to speak
> Out of Olivet the words
> Of knowledge and good-will?

These words suggest our goal: the knowledge that begets goodwill and the goodwill that seeks more knowledge. The roads may be many but the goal we know, and I can say with conviction that there is no true Canadian who is not glad to enter this high pilgrimage.

ADVENTURING IN CANADA

*At the Annual Convention of
the Association of Life Insurance Presidents, New York,
13th December, 1928.*

Mr. Chairman and Gentlemen:

I confess to you that I share fully your own
anxiety as to this part of your programme. I
am impressed by the lesson of a riddle which I
heard propounded the other day: "Why is a
diplomat like an oyster?" The answer is:
"Because the normal condition of both is
silence and when either opens his mouth he
gets into trouble!" And yet, in defiance of
the warning, I have allowed myself to be be-
guiled by your invitation here this morning.

It is an awe-inspiring experience. I recall
that on certain occasions I have found myself
quite unable to cope with the arguments of one
representative of the life insurance world who
approaches me, like David (and I am no
Goliath), single-handed, and now what am I
to do when I am confronted with all the field-
marshals and generals of life insurance on this
continent? Most of us have discovered, of

course, that the best way to approach insurance in any shape or form is in a spirit of surrender (our personal "surrender-value" is usually quite low). Whenever I am confronted by a visitor from some famous corporation who inquires after my health with a sublimation of the best bed-side manner, exhibits a tender solicitude for the welfare of my family and touches delicately and discreetly on the frailty of human life, I tremblingly seize my fountain-pen and do everything that I am told to do. And then, as the ink on the line of dots slowly dries, the sinister symptoms recede, my family seems more self-reliant than ever, and the only result appears to be a vista of robust health with an impoverished pocket-book.

However, gentlemen, to be serious, there is not a thinking man who does not welcome the increasingly important place which life insurance is taking in the modern community. The great force of to-day's salesmanship was never employed for a finer purpose than in promoting its use. The broader its application the better the state is served. I am not now speaking as a former director of a life insurance company in Canada with which my relations were both pleasurable and instructive, but I think I am voicing the view of the laymen everywhere who believe in the profession of insurance and the work which it is carrying on.

It was not always thus. The other day I came across an observation on life insurance made by Daniel Defoe, the author of "Robinson Crusoe". He remarks:

> Insuring of life I cannot admire. I shall say nothing to it but that in"—I think I had better leave the country nameless—"in Country X,—where stabbing and poisoning is so much in vogue, something may be said for it . . . and yet I never knew the thing much approved on any account.

It is a far cry from this sceptical attitude to the universal acceptance of insurance to-day and its amazing extension, particularly on this continent. As a matter of fact, we cannot escape the fact that the principle of insurance embodies the very qualities which are almost the distinguishing feature of the civilized community—a sense of foresight and the capacity for co-operation. The primitive man takes but little thought for the morrow. He is naturally a fatalist. It is the mark of the civilized being to organize for the future. But insurance, in its practice, shows more than individual prudence and foresight; it demonstrates men as social beings bearing a common burden from which each can benefit. And, furthermore, insurance illustrates these qualities of foresight and mutual aid organized into a science.

The theme has fascinated many. I have been interested in glancing at a thesis propounded by a distinguished professor at Harvard, a few years ago, in which he argues that if the principle of insurance demonstrates the interdependence of human beings within the state, why not apply it to the international sphere and give to the world a corresponding sense of interdependence and security? In Professor Royce's book, mutual insurance demonstrates the fundamentals of the "great community", as he conceived it, in which self-interest and the common good were harmonized. Many of you may know the book of which I speak. It is worth examination—this plan for the insurance and reinsurance of national personalities against all that might jeopardize their welfare.

But, whatever may be the possibilities in an international sphere, we know the facts as they apply to national communities. I have heard it maintained that the statistics of insurance are a better gauge of national progress than bank loans or even the volume of trade. It is an indication of national wealth

and also national character. But I am diffi-
dent about pressing this point because it will
appear to you that I am making a rather bom-
bastic claim for my country. For this I apolo-
gize, but on this occasion I feel in duty bound
to report to you officially that life insurance
is growing with astounding rapidity in Canada. Many of you here to-day will, of course,
know the facts. We had last year in Canada,
life insurance in force to the total amount of
over five billions. I find that the increase in
the value of policies during the twelve months
of 1927 amounted to more than the total
amount in force in 1910. The assets of Canadian companies have increased in twenty
years by over 700%. But you know that we
believe in life insurance in Canada. Possibly
the thrifty Scottish strain in our national
character has something to do with it.

Insurance has a distinctly international aspect in North America. Many of your companies, as everyone knows, are in friendly
competition with ours in Canada. Statistics
show that the home team is comfortably in the
lead. Several of our companies, on the other
hand, are well established on this side of the
boundary. I find, however, that official
records are singularly silent as to what share
of the business we actually possess. This may

be due to a wise strategy on our part which is unwilling to alarm you as to the seriousness of our invasion, or it may be due to a measure of nervous apprehension on yours. But we know that there is plenty of room for all the companies that are supplying the world with this great commodity.

As regards my subject this morning, I was allowed a dangerous amount of liberty—even permitted to conceal the theme of my remarks until I had you helpless before me. There is one subject that I felt it was not incumbent upon me to deal with, however enthusiastically I might feel on the subject, and that is the value of life insurance. I felt that somehow this audience would be sufficiently convinced of its importance and informed as to its nature to be guaranteed immunity from the uninstructed observations of a layman.

The international aspect of this occasion, however, suggests a theme on which you may bear with me for a few moments this morning. It is a subject with which you are concerned as well as I—and that is your northern neighbour. The profession of insurance itself shows our neighbourliness. You have demonstrated your confidence in Canada by investing in our country a large proportion of the profits from your Canadian business. We re-

ciprocate in kind, and we also make another
contribution to life insurance in this country
by letting you draw liberally on our supply of
insurance actuaries. I confess that my mem-
ories of arithmetic at school are still so poignant that I am always impressed by the qualities of my own country when I realize that we
can produce more members of this awe-inspiring fraternity than we can employ.

You are not without direct knowledge of
your neighbour to the north. You have en-
trusted a large sum from your savings to us.
You cannot, therefore, be without interest in
hearing what progress we are making, what
developments are forthcoming, what the
grounds are for our future confidence.

The theme of your sessions here this week
is, I notice, "Strengthening National Unity
Through Business". I have been interested in
applying in my own mind this formula to Canada, to see how our national unity has been
strengthened in the last generation by the
growth and diversification of Canadian business. Business in this modern age is the most
conspicuous form of national self-expression
and one can see the personality of a country
—can read a story of national adventure even
in the stilted pages of a blue book. Of course,
it will be said that business is only one side of

the life of a people. This is, of course, emphatically true. There is, naturally, a profound distinction between spiritual growth and material development in every community, but I think we often make our definitions too sharp. In most human beings the elements are mixed. In the national life the spiritual and the material are equally intermingled. There is something of the poet in every great captain of industry, every great leader of finance and commerce. Perhaps the president of a bank would not take it as an unmixed compliment if he were told he was a poet at heart. He would emphatically deny the allegation—and I confess that bankers in some moods habitually exhibit but meagre poetical qualities—but what I mean is obvious enough. There is no great achievement without imagination, without a soul behind it. In applying this to the national life of our Dominion one finds practical achievement and all the imagination of great venturing going hand in hand, for we find ourselves in a new Elizabethan age of discovery and exploration. Nowhere else in the world are there ten million people with the inspiration of such a gigantic task of bending nature to their will.

Applying the criterion of commerce to the recent history of your northern neighbour we

can find that great changes have taken place
within the last few decades under four heads:
stature, symmetry, outlook and co-ordination. The first of these, of course, is obvious.
Our growth has been inevitable, although in
recent years our commerce in all forms has
exceeded the most sanguine forecast. The
world knows—perhaps we have not been back-
ward in informing it—that this year we have
the greatest crop of wheat in our history, over
five hundred million bushels. As the first in
the list of exporting countries, we are now directing a golden stream of grain both east
and west to the markets of the world. The
acreage under wheat has steadily grown in the
western provinces during the last few years,
but it is interesting to notice that the growth
in acreage is out of proportion to the increase
in population. In 1870, for example, there
were two and one-fifth persons for every acre
sown to this grain; in 1928 there were two and
a half acres under wheat for every person in
the Dominion. This proportionate growth is
due, of course, to the improved methods of
agriculture and a wider use of machinery.

We have two industries, younger sisters of
agriculture, which have drawn the attention
of outside observers to themselves of late. One
of these is mining. Forty years ago our whole

mineral production was something just over ten million dollars. In 1927 it was more than twenty-four times as great, and the increase during the current year will probably be greater than the total production in 1886. In the sphere of mining we are busy discovering ourselves. The romance of the Spanish Main pales before the great treasure hunt which is proceeding in this modern age from the Ottawa River to the Arctic Circle.

The sister industry of paper has grown even more rapidly. The French Ambassador, on a visit to Canada the other day, made a picturesque reference to the Dominion when he said that much of it was like a great sheet of white paper with something—who knows what?— still to be written upon it. If this be true, it is perhaps appropriate that we should have become the first producer of white paper in the world. As a matter of fact, we export more of it now than all the rest of the nations combined. In 1927 the value of our paper exported was greater than our total exports of cheese, butter, fruits, cattle, fish, furs, gold and silver. Fifteen years ago the same export equalled only about one-quarter of the cheese alone which we, as a dairy country, exported. The growth of this industry has been most romantic. In 1890, just thirty-eight years ago,

Canada commenced to export pulp and paper products. In the last fiscal year over $284,000,000 worth of wood, wood products and paper left the country.

I think, however—as I know you will agree —that mere growth in stature is less significant than symmetry in growth. The diversification of industry is the surest sign of national strength and corresponds to versatility in a human being. The more things you can do the more efficient you are. It is interesting to realize how short the time is since we were almost entirely a producer of raw materials. In the last six years the increase in the export of manufactured and partly manufactured goods exceeds by over fourteen millions the increase in the export of raw products. The total of the former in 1927 was between 20% and 25% greater than the total of the latter. Agriculture formerly held an undisputed place as Canada's chief single source of wealth, and the value of the wheat exported still far exceeds the value of the exports of any other one commodity. But the recent developments in manufacturing and mining are enabling these industries to contest that position. The output of Canadian factories is not only increasing with great rapidity but, with improved methods, the growth of manufacture per capita of the population is very striking —from $89 in 1901 to $314 in 1925. From 1901 to 1927 the imports into Canada of manufactured goods have grown by just under 500% while exports of the same class of goods have increased by over 600%. A specific example of this growth in factory products is to be found in the pulp and paper industry. Under this head there is a steady increase in the form of pulp and finished paper, whereas there has been a dcrease in the export of raw material—pulpwood itself.

We have vast deposits of coal in Canada. The one province of Alberta contains 16% of the coal reserve of the world. Our great distances, the greatest handicap which we have to cope with, have hitherto prevented us from making full use of this treasure. The march of science will, in time, solve the problem. The distillation of coal into liquid form has now reached a practical stage. When it is fully developed the practice of burning raw coal will seem as crude and ineffective as the old-fashioned mill wheel is in contrast with the modern turbine, and there is no reason to doubt that this vast supply of over a million million tons will some day literally flow into Canadian furnaces.

If nature has not been kind enough to place

our metals near our greatest coal reserves, except in a few instances, we have striking compensations. The great industrial expansion in England was made possible by the proximity of coal and iron. We have found, alongside the "white coal" of the waterfall, not iron so much as other metals, and the process of electric smelting of nickel and copper and other non-ferrous metals is reproducing in the great north of Canada the happy and fortunate union of fuel and metal which made the greatness of industrial Britain.

The growth of our commerce has widened our outlook. It is interesting to find that despite the investments which Canadians are making in Canada in industrial exploitation as well as in government securities, we have found it possible to invest $1,338,500,000 beyond our shores. As a matter of fact we at present exceed the external investment per capita of our neighbour to the south. Our widening outlook is symbolized by the opening of new physical doors to the outside world. With the exception of the gateways over our southern boundary, our only outlet to the great world overseas was formerly in the east. It is astonishing, in looking over the trade statistics of the last few years, to see how wide our Pacific gateway has opened. Six years ago we shipped approximately 4,500,000 bushels of grain from our Pacific ports. Last year we shipped well over 67,000,000 bushels. This growth has been partly due to the use of the Panama Canal, partly due to the increase in our grain production in the western provinces, and has, of course, been encouraged by the increased consumption of our hard wheat in Oriental countries. Vancouver is now equipped to handle one hundred million bushels of grain in a season without undue strain. The population of Vancouver itself has increased nearly three-fold in seven years.

Another factor in our growth has been that of internal co-ordination, the communications that bind our communities into one ordered fabric. Our struggle has always been against geography. Transportation is therefore our life-blood. It is natural that we should have more miles of railway per capita than any other country in the world. We thought, a few years ago, that we were well supplied with railway mileage. We have, shared between our two great systems, over 40,000 miles of track. But new mines must be reached, new farming districts opened (1,900,000 acres were occupied this season) and new water-power developed, and this year saw the completion of nearly 800 miles of new steel, apart from the special line to the Hudson Bay.

Romance now perhaps centres in the aeroplane as the field of transportation. Canada offers peculiar opportunities for aircraft. Not only have we vast distances to be conquered and great areas inaccessible except from the air, but the innumerable water courses offer safe landing places almost everywhere for the hydroplane. This is a striking fact. Also it has been pointed out that much of the land surface of the globe borders on the Arctic Ocean and that the shortest lines between many of the world's capitals lie across our northern Mediterranean Sea. Is there not some ground for the forecast that in the future the Arctic plains of Canada will be the junction point of great airways between the continents? There is more than fantasy in the prediction made not long ago that somewhere in these northern wilds will be found a sort of "Times Square" of the air. It may be a little premature to buy real estate on the site but the thought has some substance.

May I say if you would know more of Canada, come and visit us. You will be most welcome. You will find us busy; you will find us with the enthusiasm of a country still full of pioneers. Let me close by quoting

an observation which was made not long ago
at a meeting of the Hudson's Bay Company,
which as you know once owned our great
north west and still carries on there the business of a great corporation. A question was
asked as to the wisdom of certain good investments which the company is making in
the western provinces. The answer which,
according to report, came from the Chair was
to this effect: "Two hundred and fifty years
ago a group of Englishmen commenced business in what is now Canada under the name
of 'The Governor and Company of Adventurers of England Trading into Hudson's
Bay' ". Their faith was justified and we are
still adventuring!" So, in a field commensurate with Canada itself and with an ever-
deepening confidence, we are still engaged in
our great national adventure,—confident of
our own progress, proud to be a loyal member of the great British Empire in which we
find our finest national expression; and happy
in the enduring friendship of our great neighbour.

THE ANGLER AND THE DIPLOMAT

*At the Annual Dinner of The
Anglers' Club of New York,
15th January, 1929*

Mr. Chairman and Gentlemen:

I greatly appreciate the honour of your invitation this evening. It is a genuine pleasure to meet the members of the Anglers' Club of New York. I do not mind admitting, however, that I find myself in a peculiarly difficult position. Let me confess to you at once that my relations to fish, fishing and fishermen are embarrassingly remote. Therefore, to talk about fish to this gathering of anglers, with no knowledge of the subject, would be an impertinence, even an irreverence. On the other hand, if I neglect to make decorous, respectful references to fish I should be guilty of an unseemly breach of good manners. Could any dilemma have sharper horns?

It is, I can assure you, most pleasant to be here, but I can't help asking myself the question, *"Why* am I here?" How does it happen that I have been admitted to a dinner of a fraternity of anglers, followers of a distinguished, jealously-guarded, almost mystical cult? As a matter of fact, I have several theories as to why I, a non-fisherman, am temporarily admitted to your midst. There is a hill not far from San Francisco called Strawberry Hill, the reason for the name being that no strawberries, under any circumstances, have ever been known to grow on it. (Incidentally I am told that this is an interesting sort of admission for a Californian to make). This barren eminence is no doubt pointed out by residents of that most fertile of states to emphasize the fecundity of the remaining countryside. Perhaps you have introduced into a society of Waltonians "The Incompleat Angler" by way of contrast to your own one hundred per cent. loyalty to the craft. Or perhaps I am here to-night as a sort of "death's head at the feast", a dreadful example to those who might be weakening in the faith, an exhibit of what happens when parents "spare the (fishing) rod and spoil the child". Again, perhaps I am a subject of your missionary spirit, a brand to be plucked from the burning, or lastly, it may be that this non-angling guest of yours is to be a sort of counter-irritant, an oratorical mustard plaster, to be applied to the itch to go fishing.

Although, gentlemen, I hardly know what

to say this evening, I suppose the obvious course for me to pursue in view of the recreation which you follow, and the much-abused profession to which I belong, would be to deal learnedly with certain aspects of diplomacy in relation to fishing. We are, of course, I regret to say, familiar with such headlines as "Diplomacy in deep waters" or "Diplomacy at sea", but the relation between the diplomat's art and that of the fisherman seems, at first blush at least, more remote. But, as a matter of fact, gentlemen, it is not difficult to discover points of similarity between the angler and the diplomat. It occurs to me for one thing that you pursue the most silent of sports and that I belong to what ought to be the most silent of professions. The fish, as a matter of fact was, I believe, a Pythagorean symbol of silence. There is a passage in the *Bigelow Papers* where Mr. Lowell makes an almost pathetic reference to the effigy of a fish which apparently hangs in the halls of a certain legislature, which shall be nameless, and points out how little the turbulent legislators beneath pay heed to this mute emblem of tranquillity and self-restraint. How precious is a symbol of silence in an age of noise—an epoch of strident riveters and shrieking taxi-cabs. Let me suggest a humanitarian activity for

societies of anglers—why not offer prizes?—
golden fishes would be appropriate because
gold is the metal we associate with silence—
for soundless riveters and tranquil taxis—
and dare I say it?—silent legislators! Yours
is indeed a silent sport. I have poignant mem-
ories of the effect which innocent remarks of
mine have had during a tense moment in a
companion's preliminary negotiations with a
trout. My profession used to be regarded as
carrying the tradition of silence. However,
gentlemen, the old reticences are, I am afraid,
hopelessly destroyed. Too often the modern
diplomat finds himself treading positively a
"primrose path" of garrulousness. My conscience isn't easy about it yet for each time
I accept a new and charming invitation to
"give tongue" in public, I am reminded of
the old lady whose diary so frequently bore
the cryptic letters "T. and F." that a friend
enquired what the formula meant. She tossed
her head and replied "tempted and fell!"

Another point in common. No one can deny
that fishing as well as diplomacy has a bearing on international affairs. The other day
I ventured, in some remarks I was making in
public, to suggest that it might be well if the
statesmen and high officials of the nations of
the world were to forget their jobs for a few

weeks every year and forgather with fishing
rods and golf clubs and no suggestion of
"shop". I believe if this were done that international amity would most certainly be enhanced. (I must incidentally make a confes-
sion to you. I really didn't mean to include
golf—I just had to add the golf clubs to be
safe.) Well, there is no immediate sign of
my suggestion being acted upon, but I am relieved to notice as the days pass since this in-
discretion was uttered, that I have not been re-
called, and I am hoping for the best.

But, gentlemen, to be serious, we can be
happy to know that there are little international gatherings taking place on trout
streams and salmon rivers in various parts
of the world which have a significant relation
to international understanding—an importance not to be measured. I am sure that there
are many members of your distinguished society who annually visit the woodlands of
New Brunswick, Quebec and Ontario, and that
these occasions when you meet your fellow-
anglers from Canada provide some of the
countless sources whence flow the good feeling and understanding between our countries.
And when you meet you don't talk of the balance of trade or the state of the stock market
or the development of power—you talk of fish.

And in talking of fish you find yourselves in a realm where material things don't matter much. You may weigh and measure fish (may you do so with a proper appreciation of the ethics involved) but you cannot weigh and measure fishing. It is in just such an intangible atmosphere of pleasure that human beings can achieve real amity.

You will observe, gentlemen, that although a non-fisherman, I am not an enemy of the fisherman's art—far from it. In fact, I think that my relation to fishing is not unlike the position taken by a certain royal duke in the time of George IV with regard to another historic institution which you will admit also possesses its own importance—the Church of England. You will remember that His Royal Highness said that he could not be looked upon, strictly speaking, as a pillar of the church, supporting her from within, but he hoped that he might be regarded as a flying buttress supporting her from without.

Much could be said of the relation between fishing and statesmanship. Many of you gentlemen are better qualified than I to deal with such a subject. In our part of the English-speaking world, when we think of statesmen who have drawn power and inspiration from your art, our minds naturally turn to

Edward Grey. He is the supreme example in
the modern British Empire of a great public
servant who is the greater because his roots
are struck deep in the love and knowledge of
nature. I wonder whether you know the passage in Lord Grey's autobiography where he
describes how he looked forward with child-
like enthusiasm to that Sunday in the English
spring, when he hoped to see the glory of the
tender green upon the beech wood? The full
flush of this beauty, as you know, can last only
two or three days, but as it happened some
crisis arose which kept him tied to the Foreign
Office. I suppose the cynical observer might
say that this was a very dangerous trait of
character in a great statesman—to be thinking of the woods in spring when international
situations awaited attention, and still more
reprehensible, to reveal this weakness shame-
lessly in his memoirs. Ministers of State, they
would inform us, should concentrate on blue
books rather than on green woods. We shall
not agree. There is a sanity and a wisdom and
a balance of mind which comes of a knowledge
of the green woods which fit men the more
wisely to deal with the blue books and what
they represent.

I suppose that the amateur of nature and
sport as a figure in public life is one of the

peculiar heritages of our Anglo-Saxon world. His point of view seems to belong to the American and British peoples. As Lord Grey comes to our minds as a great example of the type in our community, Theodore Roosevelt represents the same fine tradition with you. As it happens, they were friends, but there is nothing remarkable in this, because anglers everywhere are friends. These two men, one a great American and the other a great Englishman, with their passion for nature and instinct for public service, represent one of the ·many fundamental elements in our common legacy.

The sportsman in public life is often misjudged. There is an interesting passage in John Buchan's *Life of Lord Minto,* in which he quotes a remark made by a Hindu when he heard that this lover of sport, one of whose titles to fame at the time had been the winning of the Grand National as a gentleman jockey, was coming to India as Viceroy: "What can you expect when they send out as Viceroy of India a pleasant-spoken gentleman who jumps hedges?" But the pleasant-spoken gentleman, without specialized training, brought to his difficult job—as hundreds of others trained in the same school brought to theirs—qualities of honesty and chivalry and gentleness and simplicity and tolerance which are just the attributes which are begotten of true sport the world over.

There is no correspondence school to impart these qualities. This suggests another point in common between angling and diplomacy. There is no training course for the angler or the diplomat. Walton says, as you know:

> . . . . angling may be said to be so like the Mathematics that it can never be fully learned; at least not so fully but that there will still be more new experiments left for the trial of other men that succeed us.

I should like to substitute "diplomacy" for mathematics. Not because I think that mathematics can be learned—my experience is unhappily to the contrary—but because, jesting aside, there are certain elements in the art of negotiation which lend themselves no more easily to exact formulae than do the rules of fishing. Your sport and my job are one in being in the realm of art rather than in the sphere of exact science. We may thank Providence that human nature will always resist the effort of the psychologist to chart and tabulate it. Even the moods of the trout are not more elusive.

I feel it appropriate to mention at a gathering of anglers that fish have played quite a significant part in the evolution of the modern British Empire. I am not referring to the fact that fish will provide the subject of the first treaty to be signed by a Canadian diplomatic representative in Washington. As it happens, I shall shortly sign, along with your Secretary of State, a convention leading to the better production of salmon in the waters of your state of Washington and our province of British Columbia. Of course, this is not the aristocratic salmon of the Restigouche and the lower St. Lawrence which you know so well. This is a lower middle-class salmon appearing only in tin cans, the kind that we diplomats are familiar with; but I can assure you that a diplomat gets as much fun in landing a salmon treaty as you gentlemen do in landing a salmon.

But I was really referring to quite another fish. It has been pointed out that the modern British Empire is in debt to that good fish the halibut—the *hippoglossus vulgaris*—to use his fancy name. As *a diplomaticus vulgaris Canadiensis,* to invent one for myself, I am proud to be his junior colleague, for we both have interesting jobs to do in connection with the evolution of this British Commonwealth of ours. In 1923 it was thought that the time had come for the Dominions of the British Empire to sign treaties on their own behalf when the subject in question concerned them alone. It was a striking departure from prevailing custom. Someone representing the Foreign Office in London had always hitherto countersigned Dominion treaties. But it was agreed quite rightly that this was no longer appropriate and so, when a treaty had been negotiated for the preservation of the North American halibut fisheries, one of our cabinet ministers came to Washington and signed it as the sole plenipotentiary of the King. This practice was confirmed by the Imperial Conference of the same year, and as everyone knows, three years later, in 1926, the principle was established of equality between the Dominions and the Mother Country, in domestic and external matters, as members of the same Commonwealth.

The presence of a Canadian legation in Washington is the logical expression of this principle. If, however, this is logical, it is the only thing in the British Empire which is logical. My colleague, Sir Esme Howard, opened a speech not long ago with the question, "When is an Empire not an Empire?", his answer being, "When it's a British Em-

pire". You may have seen an article in a
well-known review by a foreign observer in
which the British Commonwealth of Nations
is discussed with friendliness but an over-
powering perplexity of mind, and the only
comment on the intricacies of our Commonwealth which the author makes with real conviction is when he applies the lines from Ham-
let to the Empire:

There are more things in heaven and earth,
  Horatio,
Than are dreamt of in your philosophy.

But, as everyone knows, the old British
Empire, with all its evolutions and refusal to
face logic, and its occasional creaks and
groans, is rolling along stronger than ever before. We are happy to think it so in Canada
because our belief in our Empire is deeper
than it has ever been. I have been delighted to
find so many sincere well-wishers everywhere
I go in your country. I have a profound conviction that the vast majority of human beings
amongst the American and British peoples
realize that the welfare of civilization rests on
the prosperity of these two branches of the
English-speaking world and on the maintenance of good relations between them. The

future of human society itself is supported by these two great pillars.

Well, gentlemen, I have digressed, but you will admit that this has not been inappropriate to an anglers' dinner, because angling itself is just one glorious digression. Now, I was talking about the points in common between the angler and the diplomat. I have avoided referring to another point of similarity until the very end of my remarks. It is a painful subject. I am referring to the aspersions so frequently cast on the angler's character by the more shameless of the comic papers; and to the base innuendoes which are levelled at my profession by the more unscrupulous type of journalist. We apparently have an alleged weakness in common. This weakness is suggested by the spurious invocation which has been put into the mouth of an imaginary angler, by an enemy of your craft:

> Lord, grant to me to catch a fish
>   So large that even I
> When talking of it afterwards,
>   May have no need to lie.

I wonder if you know another base libel in a story which incidentally represents the union of two great anecdotal streams and gives them a new psychological turn. A gentleman, who was not an angler, had dined rather too well, and after dinner observed on the wall of his friend's smoking-room the stuffed carcase of a gigantic tarpon. He looked at it, swayed gently on his feet, and murmured to his host, "The man who caught that fish is a dam' liar."

You are of course familiar with the sad definition of a diplomat by the seventeenth-century ambassador, Sir Henry Wotton, who said that he was "an honest man, sent to lie abroad for the good of his country". I was interested to find that Isaac Walton, the author of your "anglers' bible", had something to say on this very subject. (I would have you remember that he wrote on diplomacy as well as on fishing!) In his life of Henry Wotton he says in reply to a request for advice by an Ambassador designate:

> That to be in safety himself and serviceable to his country, he should always, and on all occasions, speak the truth—it seems a State paradox—for says Sir Henry Wotton you shall never be believed; and by this means your truth will secure yourself, if you shall ever be called to any account; and it shall put your adversaries—who still hunt counter—to a loss in all their disquisitions and undertakings.

There is, I fear, not much comfort to be derived even from this, for the grounds for being truthful are not on a very high plane. (I hasten to say that Walton is no longer a text-book for our diplomatic service).

No, gentlemen, I am afraid there is a stigma of falsehood and duplicity attached to both your craft and the fraternity to which I belong. The subject I feel is too intimate, too poignant to be dealt with in casual prose. I have therefore, in concluding these remarks, attempted to touch, in what I am pleased to call verse, upon this link between us:

THE ANGLER AND THE DIPLOMAT.

What is the bond?", you ask of me,
  "That holds these two together?
Can diplomat and angler be,
In spite of their diversity,
  Birds of a single feather?"

'Tis so; we're bound in unity,
  Like Hero and Leander.
Ours is a strange fraternity,
Forged by a common calumny,
  And unified by slander.

Why so? Because the world has done
  Its best in ways uncouth,
For generations past and gone,
To cast unjust reflections on
  Our attitude to truth.

The diplomat, so we are told,
  In dealing with a nation,
Will fight with steel or buy with gold,
But still the monster, as of old,
  Prefers dissimulation.

The fisherman,—no better he,—
  He shows the self-same wish
To utilize duplicity.
The envoy lies officially;
  The angler lies of fish.

So say they. Let them say, indeed!
  Their libel's done one good:
The more of it we hear or read,
We're drawn the closer in our need
  Of common brotherhood.

So let their allegations pass;
  (Nor let your conscience hurt you)
In measurement of trout or bass,
Or in reports on poison gas,
We serve the goddess Veritas,
  And truth's our greatest virtue!

          . . . .

But, anglers, now farewell and hail!
  My doggerel complete is.
Beside your craft, legations pale,
For you succeed where envoys fail;
Let statesmen learn your woodland trail,
  For trout are more than treaties!

RAILWAYS AND NATIONS

At the Annual Convention of the
American Association of Rail-
way Engineers, Chicago, 6th
March, 1929

Mr. Chairman and Gentlemen:

I am not sure that I should have dared accept the very tempting invitation I received from your president if I had already seen the report of your sessions last year, which later were sent me with the compliments of the association. This portentous volume of almost ecclesiastical appearance, with fourteen hundred pages of mysterious observations, proves conclusively that you are not a frivolous body, and I am afraid I, as a crass ignoramus in the sphere of engineering, can only appear before you as a flippant irrelevancy.

Why, I wonder, do you interrupt your proceedings by inviting a mere outsider to address you? It may be, of course, that the railway world in North America in conference assembled feels it necessary to have, as one minor exhibit, a representative of the travelling public. Perhaps through a fine instinct of

chivalry you gentlemen, after taking the initiative on 364 days of the year, permit a layman on the 365th to say what he likes about
you. In any event I have you at my mercy and
I can proceed to make what observations I
like about the punctuality of trains, the meals
which are served in the dining-car, the solidity
of the mattresses in upper berths, and the effect of impulsive throttles and over-emphatic
brakes. However, I am not unmindful that
the object lessons which we learn from railway men are very applicable to an after-
dinner speech—not to take on too heavy a
load in one's argument, to avoid side-tracks in
one's deliberations and above all to finish on
time. May we never forget the classic story
of the after-dinner speaker who, like an ill-
equipped railway, possessed no terminal facilities.

This is, I believe, your thirtieth annual
meeting, a significant milestone in the history
of a great organization. In reading Dr. O. D.
Skelton's *The Railway Builders* (to which I
am indebted for many of the following facts),
I was reminded that this year, too, marks the
centenary of a great achievement in the history of the railways of the world. In October
1829, as many of you know, a very significant
event took place at Rainhill in England,

which began a century of splendid development. The close of that century is marked by the accomplishment represented by you gentlemen here to-day and your colleagues in other countries. The event, you will recall, was a contest with four entries, of which the name of only one survives, "The Rocket". The prize was £500, the donors were the Liverpool and Manchester Railway, and the object to find an engine which was more than a speculative curiosity. The successful locomotive, if over six tons in weight, had to prove its ability to draw twenty tons at the frantic speed of ten miles an hour and to cover at least seventy miles a day. A startling proposal, this contest, with its almost incredible requirements. One Liverpool merchant wagered that if a locomotive actually succeeded in attaining the speed of ten miles an hour he would eat a stewed engine wheel for breakfast. He lost; and history does not record whether he complied with the terms of the bet. Perhaps that stewed engine-wheel is what we have encountered on certain occasions in lunch counters we have patronized!

When George Stephenson's "Rocket" won this famous contest, the directors of this adventurous railway made a most significant decision. They came to the conclusion that their passenger trains, as well as freight, had perhaps better be drawn by locomotives and not by horses; and so after years of experimentation and disappointment, the steam railway, just about a hundred years ago, definitely began its career of progress. The iron horse began to feel his oats. But those dangerous revolutionaries who believed in steam railways had a bad time with Parliament and with a sceptical public. And when railways came to be projected on this side of the Atlantic, farmers were frightened that their hens would lay no eggs and their cows give no milk because of the satanic noise of the new iron monsters. They were much more sensitive to noise in those days than we are now. (I wish that we could revive some of our ancestors' views on this subject). This attitude to noise gave rise to one most unfortunate incident. You will recall the story of one of your early engines named the "Best Friend". Its attendant was so annoyed by the sound of the escaping steam that he reduced it to effective silence by the simple expedient of sitting on the safety valve. The only difficulty was that the "Best Friend" blew up. I suppose the moral of the story is that even our best friends resent being made to keep quiet.

Then came the objection of the canals and

toll roads.   In all the century of its history, the railway has never lacked an adequate supply of opponents.   Strangely enough it is now faced again with its old competitor, the highway, which is now aided by the motor car. Perhaps the aeroplane soon will add its quota of problems to railway transportation.   Someone prophesied just the other day that most of your passengers were soon going to travel by air.   I may tell you that in northern Canada we have already used heavy aeroplanes for the transportation of both workmen and building materials.   But this, after all, was for use in railway construction, so that the aeroplane is still, as far as this incident is concerned, less a rival than a hand-maiden.

The early objections to railways were often ingenious.   I love to think of the Englishman, in the early days of railway trains, who said that it was a notorious fact that the brains of business men were so addled by the swiftness of the trains that they forgot what they had made the journey for and had to write home to find out.   (That explains, no doubt, difficulties which we have all encountered). But even when the railway had become an accepted fact, it still had its enemies.   It is extraordinary to think that John Ruskin's famous letter to the *Times* on the subject was

written only some forty years ago. You will
remember his charitable observations on steam
transportation. The letter runs as follows:

> My dear Sir:
> I do not write now further concerning railways
> here or elsewhere. They are to me the loathesomest
> form of devilry now extant . . . destructive of all
> wise social habits or possible natural beauty, car-
> riages of damned souls on the ridges of their own
> graves.
>
> Ever faithfully yours,
JOHN RUSKIN.

There is, I suppose, no better test of human
imagination than a great invention like the
modern railway. The people in the early
years who saw nothing but failure in the path
of its development were probably in the majority. But there were others who made embarrassing prophecies. When we look at modern time-tables we seem to have fallen very
short of some of the generous forecasts of our
ancestors who prophesied that railway trains
would run, before long, at one hundred miles
an hour. But we shall be content if the railways stand as one department of life where
speed is sacrificed for safety.

The steady growth of efficiency and comfort
over the hundred years marks a great pan-

orama of effort. In 1927 I had the pleasure
of attending that fine pageant in Baltimore,
the "Fair of the Iron Horse". I believe it
was one of the most impressive events of the
kind ever held. The whole continent is indebted to Mr. Daniel Willard and his colleagues for an achievement in which pictorial
imagination and splendid organization were
wonderfully combined. I may say that I was
glad to see at this pageant two Canadian locomotive visitors representing the railways of
the Dominion. And as a British subject I confess to a thrill when I saw as a Steam Ambassador Extraordinary from Great Britain
that great monster sent out by the Great Western Railway bearing the name which means
so much to us in the British Empire, "King
George V".

In Canada we started railway building
rather later than you and our first railway
was apparently not a very bold project. It ran
south of Montreal, ambling in a friendly sort
of way towards your growing railway system
in New York State. But it represented the
beginnings of a healthy plant, for the fourteen miles which were laid in 1836 grew in less
than a century to the 40,000 miles of line which
we possess to-day.

I fancy that there is no part of the world

where railways mean more than they do to us here in North America. Civilization on this continent can almost be said to be woven into the network of lines which gives it a warp and woof of steel. The railway, let us never forget in this age of new inventions, was the instrument which lent our material well-being a reality. Perhaps that is why it has still a peculiar romance for us. Peoples that dwell by the sea think in terms of ships; but inland communities like so many of ours, scattered over a great continent, find their imaginations stirred, not by ships which come and go but by the great leviathans of steel which thunder through the plains and mountains of this continent from the southern deserts to the Arctic plains. You will remember Kipling's poem, where he asks himself if romance is dead. This god, Romance, seemed to have gone from the earth. Modern machinery must have killed him. Could he be found on a railway? No, not there! And the verses run:

Romance!" the season-tickets mourn,
    "He never ran to catch his train,
But passed with coach and guard and horn—
    And left the local—late again!
Confound Romance!" . . . And all unseen
Romance brought up the nine-fifteen.

To us here in North America the railway
is the very embodiment of romance. The
building of the railways, the great task of extending and managing these vast corporations
are in themselves a superb work of imagination. A railway, after all, is a poem in practical form. I am not, at the moment, let me
say, thinking of the imagination which enters
into the nomenclature of Pullman cars—although I should love to meet the man who
names them. What I meant to say is that we
often fall into the mistake of thinking that the
poet is simply a man of words. He can be a
man of action as well. And the great pioneer
railways existing here in North America, in
your country and mine, reveal the very marriage of a fine vision with a wholesome sense
of concrete reality.

You, of course, can thank the railway for
your physical unity. Your forty-eight states
are knit into one whole by the 240,000 miles of
steel line which you possess. In Canada we
owe perhaps an even greater debt to the railway builder. Our communities have been more
scattered than yours, the area which they
serve is larger, and we stood in even greater
need of the unifying force which railways can
provide. A distinguished Canadian has said
that "the railway found Canada scarcely a

geographic expression and made it a nation".
It is no wonder therefore that we have built
railways until we find ourselves the second
nation in the world as far as length of line
is concerned, and in mileage in proportion to
our population, the first, for we now have a
mile of line for every 230 people. Our railway
building, as it has happened, has taken place
in a relatively short time. About fifty years
ago we possessed only some 2,000 miles of
steel. Most of it was concentrated in the central provinces, some of it down by the sea.
There was, till the 'sixties, no Canadian railway west of Lake Huron. Then came the
building. One line down to the sea brought
our Maritime provinces into the new Canadian federation. And another railway was
carried through to the coast to bring British
Columbia into the union. The building of
the Canadian Pacific is a great story in itself,
but you gentlemen know all about it. When
we Canadians need any encouragement for the
future, one of the achievements in the past
to which we can look back with reasonable
pride is the tale of how a scattered and none
too rich population of some four millions flung
a line of three thousand miles in length over
the vacant prairies and through the mountain
wilderness to make a union with a community

of a few thousand souls on the Pacific coast.
It is interesting to remember that when this
great enterprise was completed, five years before its scheduled time, the management refused to celebrate the event by driving home
the traditional golden spike. This may have
been due to the modesty which always actuates
the true engineer, or it may have had something to do with the fact that most of those
present were Scotch! In any event they said,
"We will use an iron spike just as good as
any between Montreal and Vancouver", and if
the directors had not happened to be present
at the time, that important spike would have
been driven home by a navvy, like the rest.

Just before the Great War, as you know,
came the construction of two more Canadian
trans-continental lines. Canada had already
captured the great west but it was necessary
to consolidate the position. And then in
recent years, as everyone is aware, came the
period of reorganization which has left us with
two great systems, both servants of the public,
and one owned by it.

After the war, during a momentary period
of economic depression, we thought we had
accomplished all the railway building we
would require for a long time to come. In
fact we fancied that we had anticipated the

needs of the future by many years. In view of observations to this effect which were made within the last six or eight years, it is interesting to know that when the present programme is completed we shall have actually built since the war over 4,000 miles of additional line. This, of course, is due both to the mineral discoveries in our great half-explored northern area and to the further development of our agricultural west. Now the northernmost points on our railway lines are becoming junctions for a new network of steel soon to trace its way further in the direction of the Arctic Circle and to the new ports on the Pacific on the one hand, and the ancient but newly utilized ports on the Hudson Bay on the other.

Railways are the very bones of the economic structure of Canada. They have made the unity of our nation a possibility. But they can hardly be said to belong only to the material sphere. Sixty years ago when the word "nation" came first to be used by the Canadian people, the project of a great railway was the concrete expression of a hope in the future, just as now the planning of new lines gives fresh reality to our confidence in the years to come. Of Canada it can be said that the railway is the evidence of our faith in ourselves. National consciousness in our country,

as in yours, would have been unattainable
without the physical communication and the
human relationships which are made possible
by modern transportation. Our debt to the
railway is, of course, too obvious to need comment. In its century of history it offers many
object lessons. If its beginnings were marked
by those splendid venturings which rouse our
admiration; in its maturity, too, it can teach
us soberer virtues. The railway, I think it
fair to say, was the first organization in North
America to acquire the characteristics of a
great permanent service: the attributes of discipline, *esprit de corps*—the sense of corporate loyalty to a common task. These qualities
naturally develop slowly in a new world where
personal initiative and resourcefulness are at
a premium. But the modern railway is a
"service" in the finest sense of an abused word
and we of the public are, I think, apt to take
its qualities too much for granted. An English friend of mine not long ago dedicated a
little book on his visit to this country to "My
charming guardians, the Pullman Porters of
America". It was a pretty and deserved compliment to the hospitality of the great system
of which they were the unconscious representatives. And the efficiency of the railway
world increases daily. You will forgive me

mentioning as one recent achievement in transportation a remarkable daily "run" on a line in England (supposed in legend to be a staid and leisurely country)—the 299 miles without a pause, on the Midland Railway, between London and Carlisle, which is the longest regular "non-stop run" in the world.

I have said something of the railway and its bearing on national life. What can we say about its relation to the international sphere? What is the bearing of organized transportation on the pressing question of international unity and the contact between nations? We should know something of that in North America. About forty-five railway lines cross our border. We own and operate many miles of railway on your side, and you reciprocate by the control of many on ours. Across the boundary a greater volume of passengers and freight flows than over any frontier in the world. Frontiers elsewhere seem often to resent the passage of a railway train. Those of you who have travelled in Europe since the war reasserted the aggressiveness of borders, will have often witnessed the contest between a line of steel and a psychological barrier on an international frontier. The victory so often, even in peace time, seems to rest with the frontier. I know

one very important boundary in the east of
Europe—one of those which has emerged since
the war—which is traversed in several places,
backwards and forwards, by a pre-war railway; but the frontier is victorious over the
railway, because you are locked in your carriage during the whole journey, not only to
prevent you from smuggling, but to impress
on you the fact that a new international situation has emerged. Perhaps this is why it is
arranged so often in Europe that when the
inevitable customs officer visits your com-
partment to make his search as you enter or
leave the international boundary, he should
choose an hour between three and four in the
morning. It may be that he acts on accurate
medical knowledge, realizing that the vitality
of human beings is lowest and their resistance
weakest at this time. In any event, we have
not yet practised this device on our international boundary in North America.

What, I wonder, are the future international developments of railways? Has this
venerable institution spent itself as far as
world venture is concerned? I think not.
Even as we meet here, men are discussing
afresh the possibilities of the tunnel beneath
that twenty miles of sea which runs between
Great Britain and the Continent. Africa and

the interior of Asia offer fields of endeavour for railway building as important, and as romantic too as anything in history. North and South America have still to be united by land transportation. Even the straits of Gibraltar may one day be tunnelled. As an uninstructed layman, may I suggest that no one knows whether some time even the Bering Straits will not be the scene of a union through steel between the continents of Asia and America? It is intriguing to think of a train running on a continuous line between Capetown and Buenos Aires. Perhaps these suggestions may sound visionary, but let me confess that the extension of transportation by land makes an unconquerable appeal to those of us to whom the charms of oceanic travel are more a matter of theory than of fact.

We are living in an age of transportation. Never has movement from place to place been so easy as now. Nor have human beings ever shown such a passion for movement. It seems, almost, as if the desire of everyone nowadays is to be somewhere other than where he happens to be. (A very satisfactory ambition as far as you gentlemen are concerned!) One cannot help feeling, however, that the destination is often of less importance than the "urge" to move. Contrast this era of easy transportation, when millions travel daily and mileage is defied, with the stationary world of four centuries ago. We talk of this being an age of science—the mechanical era. So it is, and a most striking characteristic of it is that it is an age of movement. Mankind has become fluid. And so it is natural that some of the finest buildings of the present day are those which might be called cathedrals of motion—the great railway stations like those which you are erecting, to the admiration of the visitor.

What is to be the consequence of this increasing fluidity of human beings? When men and women move from continent to continent as if on a local journey, what will be the result? It is not unreasonable—it is even obvious—to suppose that if *national* unity is aided by transportation the same great facilities for intercourse will help to achieve *international* concord. But this is not the whole story. Mr. Chesterton commences one of his books with the startling observation, "I have never managed to lose my old conviction that travel narrows the mind". He means ignorant travel, of course. "Many modern internationalists", so he says, "talk as if men of different nationalities had only to meet and mix and understand each other". But we know that harmony between nations can, of course, never rest on physical contact alone. An open mind must go with it.

But I must not stray from my subject into the open switch of a digression. The harmony which we desire in the modern world cannot come without the knowledge which is born of observation—of the first-hand personal relationships which transcend all frontiers. Therefore the trustees of modern transportation enjoy a great responsibility and an equal privilege. And the vast institution which you gentlemen represent does not stand only for the commerce which makes modern human existence possible, but for the growth of travel which will help to bring about an understanding world. This is perhaps one reason why we are moved by the engine whistle which echoes in the hills, the coloured signals and the plumes of vapour in the yards, and by the long receding lines of steel which vanish into mystery.

THE SERVICE OF THE STATE

Founder's Day Address at the University of Virginia, Charlottesville, 13th April, 1929

Mr. President, Ladies and Gentlemen:

I confess to some sensation of trepidation mingled with remorse in approaching you to-day. This is the season when academic communities are exposed to the peril of the itinerant diplomat, armed with a speech. Undergraduate auditors, amongst whom listening to addresses is not a favorite pastime, suffer, it is true, such invasions with fortitude and patience. Their elders, too, attend with the forbearance which is born of wisdom and courtesy. Your guest on this occasion, let me say, is disarmed by the charm of his welcome.

There is something in the soil of Virginia which makes a Canadian feel peculiarly at home. I believe a subtle affinity exists between the ancient Dominion, as your state is called, and the newer Dominion which lies to the north of your Republic. The common use of this venerable name, in itself, is a symbol of the many spiritual ties between us.

It is always of interest to British subjects in Canada to realize that in our sovereign's title for many reigns appeared the words "et Virginiae"; for Elizabeth, your great foundress, was "Queen by the Grace of God of England, France, Ireland and Virginia". And it was not for nothing that the name of your commonwealth appeared in the royal title. Time was, as everyone knows, when there were "King's Men" in Virginia when there were few "King's Men" in England. Your House of Burgesses was, I believe, for long able to boast that "it had never passed a law in derogation of the royal prerogative". Virginia became a cornerstone of a new and independent nation, but the noble part which it has played in the history of your great Republic is not incompatible with that friendly feeling for the peoples of the British Commonwealth of which British visitors are always conscious. It is not unnatural that we should add to the list of those regions which make an appeal to our hearts, the words whch once appeared in another context, "et Virginia".

It is interesting to recall that the foundations of Virginia and Canada were laid within eighteen months of each other. The permanent settlement left by Captain Smith at Jamestown in 1607 was followed in just over a year

by the establishment of Champlain's colony
at Quebec. It is not too far-fetched to maintain that from these two seeds sown on the
banks of the James and St. Lawrence rivers
have grown the two great Commonwealths,
American and British, which mean so much
to the world to-day. Jamestown was, as a
matter of fact, the beginning, in one sense,
of both. It was the germ of your Republic—
that is of course obvious. It also gave concrete form to the vision of Walter Raleigh,
who was the first to dream (to use the contemporary phrase) of an "Empire of the Bret-
agnes". Out of the experiment of Smith and
his successors developed what we have come
to call the first British Empire, which grew
for a century and a half and more, but was
not to endure because its structural principle
was not sound. And then again Virginia
played a dual part. The stormy years of the
seventh and eighth decades of the eighteenth
century, in which Virginians figure so brilliantly, not only left this nation in being—these
years, as we know, did something more. The
slowly-learned lessons of the revolution made
possible the development of a second British
Empire which was based on the new principle
of the self-government of its constituent parts.

It has been the privilege of Canada to play

a leading role in the development of the British Empire through the nineteenth century, and in the consummation of this Empire or Commonwealth in its present form. In this we had the unconscious co-operation of Virginia at many points. English common law was first introduced into our country from Virginia. In 1721, when the first court of judicature was set up in Nova Scotia, the Governor was directed by his instructions "to make the laws of Virginia the rule and pattern" for his government. Virginians did their share in the wars which made all Canada British soil. When the province of Ontario came to be set up its system of county organization was borrowed from yours. Amongst the company of loyalists who settled in British North America there were many distinguished citizens from your state. The first Attorney-General of Upper Canada, and its Chief Justice for many years, was the son of a Virginian lawyer; and the first educationist in that province was a grandson of one of your great Governors.

Above all we are indebted to you for the sons of your great Commonwealth who served as the fathers of ours. The men you sent us were your greatest and most characteristic gift. For such is the harvest for which Virginian soil has been ever famous. Your state throughout the centuries of its life has been a nursery of public men, and this university since its establishment has played the role of the cradle in that nursery. Such a function has not been unconsciously performed. I was struck to read in that famous summary which Mr. Jefferson devised, to set out the objects of his new foundation, this significant clause: "to form the statesmen, legislators and judges on whom public prosperity and individual happiness are so much to depend". What in Jefferson's mind was a theory, became before long a matter of practice, as your century of achievement has revealed. We are reminded afresh of the contributions which the University of Virginia has made to the public life of this Republic and to the world, by the tribute, as greatly merited as it was sincere, which has been paid to-day to the memory of Woodrow Wilson, one of your most illustrious sons. After all, despite the multifarious points of contact between the modern university and the community which it serves, there is still no higher service it can render than through the men on whom it has left its mark. The history of your state, and the annals of your university, inevitably tempt the visitor in your midst to consider the relation of the graduates of to-day to leadership in life in general, and in particular to that greatest of all human activities, the service of the state.

Time was when the colleges in North America existed primarily to produce potential statesmen and divines. This is often revealed as the principal aim by the charters of the old foundations. In the picturesque words of a pious benefactor of the oldest American college, the office of higher education was to give "some encouragement for the breeding up of hopeful youths for the public service of the country in future times". (The words "some encouragement" of course suggests a modest claim). Your colleges indirectly made an impression on your national life at the very moment of its emergence. One finds that of the fifty-six men who signed your great Declaration of 1776, twenty-seven, or nearly one-half, were graduates of existing collegiate establishments. A survey of your history from then on would, no doubt, reveal that college men played a significant part in shaping the future of your Republic. And now in all parts of the Anglo-Saxon world, we find that an increasing number of the men—and women too—who are guiding the destinies of their countries, have received no small measure of their equipment in academic precincts.

The dream of the ambitious college student in the eighteenth and early ninetenth century was to fit himself to take a part in the public life of his community. The abler the student, the more natural it was for him to nurse a secret vision of himself addressing the enraptured members of a legislature, or affixing his name to some state paper of guaranteed immortality. Such then was the case, but now we notice that the scene has changed. The undergraduate who looks forward to a life of politics or public administration will find himself in a small minority. One reason for this is obvious. We are living in an economic age. A century ago, when business was local and of small dimensions, when the sciences were rudimentary, and many great professions of to-day non-existent, politics pointed the way to the most interesting, the most absorbing of occupations. The adventurous spirit, who then found his ambitions most easily satisfied in political life, will now discover commensurate rewards in countless directions.

It is true, however, that vocations which strictly fall into the category of private life may have an unsuspected relationship to the service of the state. In the early and simpler days, the division between public and private life was complete. The state confined its

operations to narrow and well-defined limits.
On the other hand, private life was more private than it can be to-day. Now, however, the
margin between private enterprise and public
affairs is narrowing. As the task of government becomes increasingly diversified no profession exists which may not bear some relation to governmental action. The scientist,
the man of letters, the lawyer, the physician,
each may find himself a servant of the commonwealth, so diversified are the activities of
government. Just as we found that war demands the energies of an entire nation in all
its departments, so does the administration of
a great country in time of peace now cover
every field of human activity. The modern
state is so complex that no member of it can
regard himself as quite detached from an active concern in its affairs. No citizen, however humble, but is part of the very fabric
of his community.

However great the contribution which can
be made to the state indirectly, nothing, of
course, can ever replace the function which is
performed by the public servant. Politics and
the public services offer careers which are no
less important because of leadership in other
spheres of activity. Quite the contrary. Society will always stand in need of men fit to

administer and legislate, who can make laws
and apply them. The modern community
everywhere relies increasingly upon those of
its members who can provide the necessary
link between the experience and knowledge at
their disposal, and the interpretation of that
experience and knowledge in concrete meas-
ures for the public good. The call the world
over is for men with the gift and the vocation
for the service of the public weal.

This will appear as a sententious platitude,
but I have noticed that my own young friends
accept it as a platitude only in its theoretical
aspects. As a practical proposal it seems
to many startling and revolutionary. A life
of public administration or a career in politics
appears somehow remote and unreal to the
undergraduate of to-day. In modern life, of
course, as I have suggested, the greatest rewards for men in influence and power seem to
be offered in the sphere of finance and industry
and the related professions. This is particularly true of our newer world, where the first
golden age of economic development has not
yet closed. Again, in countries which are comparatively young, it is only in times of rare
crisis that political issues are fundamental
and overwhelming to the exclusion of all else.
In the old world, where economic pressure is

inexorable, and historic issues ever present, the service of the state is a natural medium of self-expression for the active mind. There the relation between political action and the individual is closer and more vividly felt. In the more comfortable and spacious atmosphere of the western hemisphere, how easy it is for us to regard the public service as someone else's job, or to look on the business of government as automatic, like the marvels of machinery in present-day industry, and to think of society's progress as moving according to mathematical formulae.

It is surely true of all ages as well as of all places that politics, rightly conceived, offers the greatest sphere of leadership in human affairs. We are happy to do honour, of course, to those who have achieved fame in this great vocation, we even envy them their eminence. But with that inconsistency which is true of human nature we are too often content to conceive our own political obligations as being satisfactorily discharged, when we pass final judgment on the work of those who are bearing the heat and burden of the day in parliament or council chamber, while we enjoy a comfortable immunity from the ardours which they undergo, without perhaps even discharging the easy responsibility of the suffrage.

Goldwin Smith once said "politics is the noblest of all callings and the meanest of all trades". Be it viewed as trade or calling, there is no question as to what it is, viewed rightly. No finer career is given the youth who leaves the university with high aims and rich promise than to serve as the interpreter between the ideal standards of the class-room and the maximum possibilities of active life. But we cannot conceive such a career only in terms of the lustre which is shed on the figure of the elder statesman. Such eminence is given to few. "Statesman" is a title but sparingly bestowed. Every community the world over must honour those who are prepared to serve it, perhaps in relative obscurity, and under the hardship of occasional misunderstanding and even obloquy in the sphere of what we call public life. We are inclined to neglect the importance of the art of politics, the technique of political action. This function is just as essential to the state as the principles of government themselves, for the statesman who possesses ideas and does not know how to apply them is as ineffective in a political sense as the politician with no ideas to apply. Democracy is never more unreasonable than when it is indifferent to those whom it has chosen to act as the trustees of its corporate welfare. The university is never more closely in touch with the well-being of the state than when its sons are prepared to assume such trusteeship for no reward other than the honour of serving.

But I have suggested that the service of the state is not limited to those who are in public life. The youth, for example, who decides upon a career in the world of trade has by no means robbed himself of opportunities for public leadership. The great corporation the world over is assuming a position in the community in which its own welfare is rightly regarded as commensurate with that of the body politic. Generations ago the man of business was looked upon as having an interest apart from, and even opposed to, that of the state. The greater the corporation, the greater it was often thought was the menace to the public weal. Big business seemed often to be inevitably bad business. Now happily there is a change. This may be due no doubt partly to the widening diffusion of ownership. There is another reason which is, I believe, more profound. The attraction of men of education into business has brought a significant result. The man of trained mind and quickened sense of responsibility cannot regard his work as an isolated thing with no relation to the life of

the community of which it is a part. He will
study it in terms of its proper setting, will be
able to see it in true perspective. The leaders
of industry and finance of to-day are increasingly the kind of men whose sense of obligation to the state has developed with the power
which they wield. They show us that statesmanship need not be confined to the sphere of
government, for the leader in the business
world, through his own qualities and the
growth of business itself, finds himself more
and more in the position of a public servant.
And this is true of all great vocations in modern life. No real leader in any sphere of activity can be other than a leader of the community in which he works.

The world asks for leaders in all its varied
fields. One function of the modern university
is, surely, to give the answer in concrete form.
I was much struck, not long ago, in coming
across an observation by Mr. Woodrow Wilson who asked, in one of his essays, the significant question, "What is the college for?",
and his reply was this: "It is the training of
men who are to rise above the ranks." It
sounds at first blush like a natural answer to
a simple question. We may agree with facility
to the reply, but I wonder whether we actually
are prepared to accept all the implications of

what Mr. Wilson said. If men are to be
trained to rise above the ranks, if democracy
is to be given leaders by the college, is the
college facing its task? What endowment can
four years of what we call higher education
leave to the graduate, which will help him to
act as a leader of the rank and file?

If the university is to train men who will
rise above the ranks it is obvious that its task
is not only one of education but also, and primarily, one of selection. If the hundreds of
thousands of graduates who pass annually
into the world to-day were all to serve as
leaders, one might almost feel that society
would resemble a certain army whose officers
slightly outnumbered the privates. The problem nowadays which the colleges are facing is
how to discover the student of promise as
early as possible, and then to give him an education, not shaped to the capabilities of the
many who are now admitted so easily to the
privileges of higher education, but to give him
a training commensurate with his capacity.
That suggests one of the greatest problems of
modern higher education—the problem of
numbers. The college of liberal arts has been
forced by the size of its enrolment to assume a
dual responsibility. It must, of course, do its
best for the flocks of those who wish to live in

a collegiate atmosphere for a time without un-
due intellectual strain (and their rights are
by no means to be ignored). But this function must not be allowed to impair the chances
of those who can benefit from a more thorough
and exhaustive education. There is one familiar plan, in force as it happens in my own
university as well as in some of yours in this
country, by which those students who are not
content simply to absorb what we are pleased
to call "culture", as it were, through the pores,
but are capable of genuine intellectual effort,
are required to read for honours in carefully
prescribed intensive courses, while their fellows looking to a pass degree, follow a less
exacting and more discursive curriculum.
This system makes an appeal to me, for it
helps us to escape from a sad misrepresenta-
tion of democracy which has been no friend
to modern education. The theory, which we
accept, that political power should spring
from all alike, does not imply that all possess
equal attainments. The ends of democracy
are best served when it trains those best fitted
to govern and places them in authority. There
is a mine of wisdom on this subject, which has
not escaped the attention of the modern
scholar, in a book written more than three
centuries ago by the English humanist, Sir

Thomas Elyot, in which he endeavoured to
give his views on the education of the leader
or, as he called him "The Gouvernour". The
good Sir Thomas knew that the raw material
of governors was not uniform.

> Beholde", he says, "also the ordre that God hath
> put generally in al his creatures, . . . and it may nat
> be called order, excepte it do contayne in it degrees,
> . . . And therefore hit appereth that God gyueth nat
> to euery man like gyftes of grace, or of nature, but
> to some more, some lesse, as it liketh his diuine
> maiestie.

It is amongst those men with especial "gifts
of grace", as Sir Thomas puts it, that we
must expect to find our potential leaders in the
university.

What of their training? Sometimes in the
rich confusion of modern life, with the danger
of confounding end with means, of seeing the
part as greater than the whole, we must reduce things to their elements to understand
them. I am interested in a movement in
Great Britain which has stripped education
to its stark realities, and has a lesson for those
of us who have enjoyed, and rightly enjoyed,
the accessories with which it has been embel-
lished. When the system of tutorial classes
for working men, now known as the Workers'

Educational Association, was set up in England, with its rigorous exacting three-year course in a well-defined field of learning under able teachers, the question was asked: What diploma or degree or certificate would be granted at the end of the period? What tangible reward would the student gain for the hours of intense and conscientious study which followed a hard day's work in the mine or factory or railway? But the grim north countrymen who formed the first classes refused, with an academic asceticism, to accept any external recognition—to them hard intellectual effort itself was its own reward. As for the equipment of their training, this was nothing other than the greatest equipment of real education since teaching began—the teacher himself.

What shall be taught? It may seem like heresy to suggest that not even knowledge itself is the aim of the training of the leader. The acquisition of knowledge must, of course, be the principal aim of those in a professional school; the pursuit of learning must be the object of the great schools of research; the diffusion of information a corporate task assumed by the modern university. But for the student in the college of liberal arts receiving from the humanities what they can give him, we know that what he learns is of less importance than how he learns it. A liberal education, as has been said, is what you retain after you have forgotten all you learned. The superstition, of course, persists that the stores of facts with which one comes away from college are in themselves of significance. A retentive memory it is true is a priceless gift, but the student will find that the habits of mind which are formed are what matters: the ability to acquire knowledge, to discover the essential thing, to relate it to life. Learning by itself can be inert and lifeless. As someone has observed, "Knowledge does not keep any better than fish".

What, one may ask, is the best mental pabulum of the undergraduate? What content is most likely to fit him for his role of leadership? An important question in a negative sense, because of the time we can waste through miscalculation, and yet the course of study may be of little significance as a means to an end. It is probably a tribute to our faith in education that we regard the curriculum as a creative force in itself. Schools of government are of undoubted value in equipping the future public servant with the technique of statecraft and administration. *Ad hoc* courses in journalism and business administration and diplomacy, all have their uses, but I would suggest that they can be no substitute for the mental discipline and humanizing influence of studies which are remote from the sphere of professional technology. Not only may such studies be remote, but I would suggest that they *should* be remote from the materials of one's future calling. I was deeply impressed by an epigram on this subject in the writings of one of your distinguished educationists. In referring to the content of liberal education, he said, "Depend upon it that the sword is best whetted on that which it is never destined to cut". As to what is the best whetstone of the mind, I have no prescription to offer. The classics have an honourable place in the training of many great men in your country and mine. I suspect their influence was greater before the science of philology asked us to approach them as languages rather than as literature. (But I must not enter controversial ground.) I was looking the other day at the requirements for the examination for admission to the Indian Civil Service of Great Britain. This service, as everyone knows, for generations has been charged with the task of administration in a most complicated country, which demands technical knowledge of a highly exacting nature. It is interesting to see that the candidates for admission to this distinguished body of experts in Indian finance and law and public administration, are not required to exhibit a knowledge of these things in the first instance (that, of course, must come later). Rather must they show themselves in the first place competent in the use of English and in a knowledge of contemporary affairs. And secondly, their general intellectual capacity is demonstrated by proficiency in such apparently remote subjects as moral philosophy or metaphysics or Latin and Greek or pure mathematics. An eminent American diplomat, in writing a few years ago of the education for his profession, deplored the neglect of the classics because of their value in giving the student a sense of accuracy of expression, and proceeded to make the striking comment —that much of whatever misunderstanding existed between the two North American neighbours in the nineteenth century, was a result of the unnecessary ambiguity in certain treaties due to their untidy draftsmanship. On this observation I shall refrain from making any comment; but we may agree that there is no more valuable gift which a college can bestow upon its sons than the capacity to use their native language with force and lucidity.

Clear expression, it is of course a truism to say, cannot be dissociated from clear thinking —the one almost inevitably implies the other. The wise educationist knows that this faculty cannot be acquired by the external application of some curricular varnish, it must be in the very warp and woof of the educational scheme. When my friends tell me of some miracle to be performed by a new addition to the plethora of college courses already existing, I am reminded of the well-intentioned efforts of a distant nation, which shall be nameless, to improve the reputation of its citizens in the world of trade by introducing into the national schools a new subject, with appropriate text-books, known as "Commercial Honesty".

A college in which I lived for several years bore as its motto the old legend *Abeunt studia in mores*. It is of course, after all, the unconscious transmutation of studies into habits which makes their selection of such significance. Even the mental discipline and intellectual capacity bequeathed by a few years' companionship with the humanities are of less importance than the orientation of mind which a liberal education should give us. If the university is to supply men who are to rise above the ranks, it must endow them with

certain qualities. May I suggest two attributes which the university should stand for and
with which it should endow its sons, if they are
to be leaders. First, it must stand for *quality*.
Its graduates must possess a sense of quality.
They must be the friends and not the foes of
distinction. They must, whatever their
sphere, be uncompromisingly intolerant of the
second-best. They must set for themselves an
inexorable standard of achievement. The
word quality, of course, possesses a faint
aroma of an order of society which we have
rejected. The world is still in reaction against
an age in which privilege outlived obligation,
and mere station survived the merit which had
perhaps once justified it. But we need not dis-
card all the attributes of a superseded era.
The graces need not be condemned with the
faults. Above all shall we remember that in
the case of the true aristocrat privilege en-
tailed responsibility. Nowhere can we be
more conscious of the privilege conferred by
the university on its sons, than in this place
of natural loveliness and historic beauty which
enshrines so great a tradition of achievement.
With such privileges our colleges bequeath a
legacy of equal obligation.

The phrase "aristocracy of brains" may
suggest itself, but this has unfortunate impli-

cations, for the prig and the pedant are, of course, education's worst enemies. Even an honest philistine is less dangerous. Mr. Asquith in an immortal phrase once ironically asked why the members of a certain college were so endeared to the hearts of their fellows, and conjectured that it was because of their "tranquil consciousness of effortless superiority". We have learned but little of our Alma Mater if our learning does not possess the leaven of humility.

The sense of quality, so essential to academic leadership, will find its balance in another legacy of the college to its sons: a sense of *proportion*. Society suffers less it would seem from the absence of virtue than from the emphasis of one virtue to the neglect of others. It is the task of a liberal education to help us to see life in true proportion, so that we can find our love of knowledge balanced by a feeling for humanity, and so that while being a friend of man in the abstract, we do not forget to be the friend of men. It will help us to avoid the high thinking without hard thinking, which is sentimentality, and the hard thinking without high thinking, which is materialism. It will help us to see our work in terms of the community, and our nationality in relation to mankind. Its product is the

man of disciplined mind and broadened sympathies and quickened imagination, generous
yet discerning, uncompromising albeit gentle.
It will give us, in the words of an Elizabethan
prayer, "a spacious outlook into the world".

THE ARTS AND NATIONALITY

At a Dinner Given by the American Academy of Arts and Letters in Celebration of the Twenty-fifth Anniversary of its Foundation, New York, 23rd April, 1929

Mr. Chairman, Your Excellencies, Ladies and Gentlemen:

As a junior diplomat let me confess that I am somewhat overawed at being plunged suddenly into the society of a roomful of academicians representing the erudition and scholarship of this great country. I am uncomfortably haunted by the thought of the split infinitives which may be found lurking in despatches which I have signed, and by the false quantities which may have slipped into Latin quotations which I have been rash enough to employ. I am only comforted by the fact that charity is an essential attribute of true learning.

Seriously, however, let me tell you, sir, how greatly honoured I am to be here to-night at your generous invitation and to join in the

celebration of the twenty-fifth anniversary of
the foundation of this most distinguished
body. I feel confident in extending to you
the cordial greetings of Canada on the completion of this quarter-century of brilliant
accomplishment, that I am expressing the profound admiration of everyone in my country
who has a feeling for high achievement in the
world of literature and art. We offer you,
sir, our warmest and sincerest felicitations.

This, I understand, is the anniversary of the
actual date of your establishment. I have
been wondering whether your founders were
under the subtle and insidious influence of
British propaganda when they were led to
select St. George's Day as the day of your
foundation. But we have been reminded,
ladies and gentlemen, that this is also another
anniversary, the day which is celebrated as
the birth of Shakespeare, three hundred and
sixty-five years ago. Therefore, the day not
only represents national traditions to some of
us, it represents a link between our respective
nations. Shakespeare's genius is equally
yours and ours. He belongs to everyone who
speaks the English language. Although we
have bowdlerized his work and sentimentalized his person, and neglect to produce his
plays and forget to see them when they are

produced, we continue to honour his memory as a symbol of our common legacy.

It can hardly be said that we speak Shakespeare's language. Its rich exuberance and individuality are not for a generation whose vocabulary is gradually being shaped to words which fit the headline. We seem more and more to express our thoughts nowadays in terms of fixed formulae. However, notwithstanding the perils of the conventions which are forming and fixing our English tongue, it still remains an astonishingly virile thing, accepting amiably the invasions from vaudeville and the sporting page, but nevertheless being ultimately, I believe, enriched therefrom.

One sign that there is life inherent in the tongue we speak is the fact that on both sides of the Atlantic words gradually acquire a different significance. Transatlantic visitors find many snares and pitfalls in this fact. An English friend of mine confessed to me not long ago, that in addressing an audience in North America, he had said in a very friendly moment, "I am conscious, ladies and gentlemen, that I am speaking to a very homely people." He was amazed and perturbed at the effect which his innocent compliment had on the audience. He was unaware that the word which to him meant "home-loving" to those living in North America had come to mean "plain of feature".

The art of language, like all art, must of course follow national lines. One is tempted to speculate, particularly on an occasion such as this, held under the aegis of a distinguished body representing the arts and letters of a nation, how closely art and nationality are allied. It is not a new theme and it is a vast one, but I may say for your comfort that although I recognize that "art is long", I am equally conscious that in post-prandial utterances it must be remembered that "time is fleeting".

Nothing, let me say, is more fascinating to one who is for a time a stranger in your midst (and your friendliness and hospitality have made me feel anything but a stranger) than to watch the exuberant development in this country of the arts in every field. It would be an impertinence for a visitor to attempt to analyze the elements of your achievements, let alone to appraise them. Your accomplishments are as significant as they are diversified. For instance, as a lover of the theatre I am struck by the fact that here this historic institution is being reclaimed from the limbo to which the Anglo-Saxon mind had condemned it. The theatre is being saved from being exclusively a place of recreation for those members of the community who, as legend has it, are perpetually tired, and is gradually becoming a vehicle for the expression of ideas and a meeting ground for the arts. Again let me say that as an amateur of architecture, I am amazed, like thousands who come to your country, by the achievements of the members of that great profession which one finds so eminently represented in this distinguished body. Here in this city the engineer and the artist have combined to produce a new architectural form—no inconsiderable feat. The living towers which now enrich your skyline represent a transformation which sometimes seems to have been made almost overnight— when one approaches one's hotel of a year ago and finds on its site a soaring office building. And so, in countless ways, one is filled with admiration at what is being done here in literature and the arts, and on a sound national basis in accordance with the true background and traditions of your Republic.

My country is younger than yours and we are at an earlier stage of economic development, but with us too, the arts are expressing national life. Canada is not only represented by wheat fields and mines and forests—im-

portant though they are—or by the feats of
engineering which are poetry in themselves,
but in things you cannot weigh or measure
we are making our own progress. Our arts
and literature, like yours, are true to our national setting. In painting, for instance, we
are influenced increasingly by the brilliant
colour and vigorous design of our own north
country. Our painters have abandoned the
irrelevant inspiration of exotic subjects and
have set themselves to the task of painting
what they see about them with a directness and
honesty which have already borne their fruit.

The growth of the arts in North America
has therefore moved step by step with the development of self-consciousness in our neighbouring nations. This, however, is no new
phenomenon. This is just what happened, as
we know, over the years in Europe. The nation, after all, has been the very workshop of
art. Most of the borrowed beauty which we
have brought from another world to enrich
our modern life here in this continent has been
produced through the travail of nations
through the centuries. Nationality, however,
whatever may be its gifts or virtues, has been
under searching criticism since the Great
War. Its excesses have naturally met with
disfavour, but they have also led to attacks on

nationality itself. We have people about us who look on a nation as a force inherently unprogressive and even evil. A lady was reported to have observed not long ago, "I have no sense of nationalism, only a cosmic consciousness of belonging to the human family." I do not know what cosmic consciousness means, but if it means the destruction of those qualities of mind and custom which make one nation different from another and give variety and colour to life, then I would suggest that "cosmic consciousness" is a bad thing to get!

Art itself, after all, ladies and gentlemen, is the very refutation of the cosmopolitan idea. It is the most national thing in life. But, paradoxically enough, it is the most international thing. We need not be reminded that there is no society in which international asperities are so soon forgotten as those concerned with the arts and letters. Art, after all, is a kingdom in itself. It is a unifying, not a dividing force. Human beings are separated by material things only; they are essentially united by the spiritual.

There were times, so historians tell us, when the early painters and sculptors of Europe enjoyed especial privileges even when wars were raging. But one need not go very far back in history for an illustration of the immunity of the artist. Samuel Morse, the inventor of the electric telegraph, and a distinguished American both in science and in art, was in England during the war of 1812, and although he was technically at the time an alien enemy, it is interesting to recall that he was publicly presented with a medal by a society of artists for his achievement as an amateur painter.

The world is concentrating, as never before, on the abolition of war through the creation of relationships which will make such disasters impossible. It has been wisely pointed out, however, that although the minds of men may now be against war their feelings are not yet proof against its appeal. In other words, we have realized that war is a stupid and irrational business but our emotions are still dangerously open to the glamour which can be made to surround it. Peace beside it may seem relatively dull. But if peace is looked on only as the absence of war it of course is a mere negation, and nothing can be built on a negation. The atmosphere of peace, it seems obvious, must be made to possess a romance of its own and thereby enabled to command both the feelings and minds of human beings. It must be active rather than passive. War, we know, has qualities which can be dramatized. It would be well to know how to dramatize peace. Perhaps the diffusion through the world of an interest and participation in the arts and the wider popular concern in fine things will do more than we know to endow peace, in theory as in practice, with the lustre it should possess. I hold no brief for the originality of such a view. We have heard it expressed before. But although we may express it, do we accept it?

The day will come when a sense of beauty will pervade society and art will be neither a digression from the business of life nor an enervating luxury for the few, but the normal possession of the crowd. When art belongs to the many it will become not only material for the occasional self-expression of the individual, but more and more a form of national self-expression. One can conceive of art as a reasonable sphere for healthy, national rivalries to occupy. A few months ago two destroyers steamed up the Thames with a strange cargo, under escort. They were the convoy of a ship carrying the greatest collection of paintings which had ever left the shores of the Netherlands. For weeks, as everyone knows, Burlington House in London was thronged with delighted crowds visiting this exhibition. It happens that the last time an expedition from Holland lay in an English river was two centuries and a half ago, when the guns of a Dutch admiral were heard in St. Paul's churchyard. These two invasions of Great Britain from the land of Rembrandt offer a striking contrast and suggest international possibilities on which there is no need to enlarge.

To the problem of peace, ladies and gentlemen, the arts have their proper contribution to make. If it has been said that with the advance of art peace will find a surer footing, the statement is no mere extravagance of rhetoric. When a natural sense of beauty captures us and our community ministers to that sense, life will be richer and men will be wiser. Then it is not too fantastic to suppose that our outlook on the world may be in a truer perspective and that we may, in a familiar phrase, be able to "see the parts as parts but with a feeling of the whole".

CATHEDRALS
IN THE TWENTIETH CENTURY

*Before the National Cathedral
Association at Washington
Cathedral, 9th May, 1929*

Mr. Chairman, My Lord Bishop, Ladies and
Gentlemen:

I may say for your comfort that when
Canon Stokes and I considered the length of
the remarks which I was so kindly invited to
make this morning, we agreed, with a satisfactory unanimity, that they should be brief.
I am glad, however, to have the privilege of
foregathering with the members of the National Cathedral Association to-day. No one
who is a resident in Washington for a time
can help being grateful to the men and women
here and throughout this country who are
making possible the erection of the great
cathedral church which is slowly rising above
this city. To those of us who have been nur-
tured in the English tradition this corner of
your capital makes a peculiar appeal. As it
happens there is an especial affinity between
your cathedral church and that of the diocese

in which I live, because the latter bears the
name which is so familiar in your cathedral
close—that of St. Alban, the proto-martyr of
Britain. But apart from that the quiet gardens, the grey walls with an occasional touch
of Gothic sculpture, and the clustered buildings in mediaeval style which are rising everywhere on this hillside, together with the great
edifice which crowns the whole—all this suggests the atmosphere of the little island of the
North Sea which we in Canada affectionately
call the "Old Country".

There are people, of course, who regard a
modern cathedral as an anachronism. They
tell us that the age which expressed itself in
the great buildings which sprang up in England and in France through the twelfth and
thirteenth centuries has passed; that modern
life is symbolized more accurately by structures of another sort, by the great bridges, the
dams and the soaring buildings which are the
triumph of the present-day engineer. I remember a few years ago having some hours
to spend in the city of Liverpool, when I
thought I would pass the time by visiting the
new cathedral which is slowly taking form
there under the genius of Sir Gilbert Scott.
I knew I would find a structure possessing
great beauty, but I felt that it might be found

to bear a rather artificial relationship to its
community. I discovered to my surprise that
my apprehensions were ill-founded. One has
only to walk through the choir and chapels
of this splendid building and see the people
of all classes thronging it, and to watch the
folk from the country and the shawl-covered
women from Liverpool, dropping their pen-
nies into the boxes as a contribution to the
completion of the fabric, to realize that Liverpool cathedral is a genuine and natural and
honest expression of the feeling and aspirations of the people of West Lancashire. It
has become a people's cathedral.

Here in the United States you too are building cathedrals. A magnificent structure is
rising on Morningside Heights in New York,
which will be a great possession of your larg-
est city; and here in Washington, the capital
of the Republic, you have chosen one of the
most beautiful sites in the world on which to
build a cathedral church which will be one
of the finest treasures of this country and an
inspiration to all who come to see it. Already
your cathedral close with its splendid gardens
possesses unforgettable charm.

The building of a cathedral, far from being
an enterprise which is irrelevant to modern
life is, it seems to me, a singularly appropriate

object for our attention. And for this may be
suggested several reasons, some of them obvious and some of them less so. For one thing,
the cathedral is a symbol of scientific achievement. The sceptic who tells us that such
things are out of date, that we are living in an
age of science which has no place for cathedral
building, forgets that the mediaeval cathedral,
although a thing of beauty was also a triumph
of engineering. The subject has been, unfor-
tunately, sentimentalized. I am afraid we
cannot acquit John Ruskin of having given
the world a misleading conception of this
achievement of the middle ages. In his finely-
written chapters on the glories of great
churches he approaches his subject as an
artist, and thinks almost exclusively of the
romantic aspect of architecture. When, under
his influence, we liken the interlacing arches
and the vaulting of a cathedral nave to a glade
in the forest, it is not difficult to fall into the
error of thinking that the builders of the
mediaeval church had such a simile in mind
when under their skill this form was developed
and perfected. The English architect, Sir
Thomas Jackson, some years ago published
a book called *Reason in Architecture,* which
applies a healthy corrective to this sentimental point of view. The author points out

that the mediaeval builders, like all builders,
were reluctant to depart from familiar types
of architecture They had been accustomed,
for instance, to a roof in the form of a simple
barrel vault supported on walls thick enough
to carry its weight, and pierced by the prevailing round-headed windows. It became
necessary to economize in material and to
build thinner walls, and when the art of making good mortar was gradually lost, the great
weight of the roof had to be supported by some
other means than that of an inert mass of
masonry. So the principle of counterpoise
was gradually developed, and a long process of
experimentation led to the adoption of the
groined vault which concentrated its thrust
on the great pillars of the nave, which were in
turn supported by smaller vaults in the aisles
and outside piers and flying buttresses,
weighted by pinnacles, until the whole familiar
machinery of the mediaeval church was employed and even the pointed arch, the most
characteristic feature of what we call the
Gothic style was, as we learn, reluctantly
adopted in the first instance as a necessary result of the solution of engineering problems.
There is a passage in Jackson's book which
throws an interesting light on this question:

It would surprise many people, as they stand in the silence of some great Gothic minster, whose ancient stones seem to have grown old in peaceful calm and slumberous quiet, if they were to realise the truth that so far from everything being at rest around them they were surrounded by mighty unseen forces engaged in active combat, thrusting and counter-thrusting one another in fierce encounter, a never-ending conflict that never slackens between antagonists that never tire . . .

I have suggested the scientific significance of the cathedral. It is less necessary to suggest its other functions. Perhaps in this day when human invention is doing so much to penetrate the unknown, and even seems occasionally almost to defeat time and space themselves, it is well that we should have places still left to give us the element of mystery. Chartres and Salisbury and Amiens and Winchester may have been the expression of an age vastly different from ours, but they represent a fundamental element which has no limitation of time; and the glory of the colour of a great east window and the soaring beauty of the lines of a Gothic nave, seen in an atmosphere of serenity and stillness so rare in modern life, represent an influence which belongs to no one age. It is perhaps more needed now than ever before.

However, ladies and gentlemen, it is not my intention to usurp the function of the architect of the cathedral in describing its construction, still less that of the Bishop in telling of its function. My purpose to-day is much simpler, merely to express to you in these few remarks the feeling of pleasure which at least one sojourner in your midst experiences in seeing what you are accomplishing here on St. Alban's Hill, and, secondly, to congratulate you on the generous scale of what you are doing. You are applying to your great edifice what Wordsworth said of the chapel which Henry VI gave to King's at Cambridge:

> High Heaven rejects the lore
> Of nicely-calculated less or more.

and future generations will be grateful to you.

TASTE

Founder's Day Address at Mount Holyoke College, Massachusetts, 8th November, 1929

Madam President, Ladies and Gentlemen:

My wife and I greatly appreciate the opportunity of visiting Mount Holyoke. This Foundation, I understand, is the pioneer institution in the United States, if not, indeed, in the world, to offer to women the advantages of higher education. The name under which you existed in the earlier years of what will soon be a century of achievement, suggests in itself your antiquity. That forbidding phrase, "Female Seminary", appearing in your original designation, seems now to conjure up a very remote past. It suggests orderly ranks of well-disciplined pupils in gingham apron and flannel petticoat, who lived to accept meekly the prevailing rules of virginal piety and domestic obedience. But practices may change while principles endure. There may be a contrast between what is done now at Mount Holyoke and what was done in the time of Miss Mary Lyon, in such matters as the

hours of rising, the household tasks demanded
of the undergraduate and the observance of
the Christmas festival (which in New England seems in the early years to have been
dedicated to the mortification of the flesh).
But the high principles of education established here by your great foundress still stand
and Mount Holyoke remains, in all essentials,
faithful to the noble ideals under the inspiration of which it was established.

My remarks this morning, if they possess
sufficient unity to justify a title, are on the
subject of taste. May I say that this all-em-
bracing topic does not suggest that I am about
to transmit to you my personal observations
on the autumn styles, or to offer hints on home
furnishing, or to give you a discourse on a
visit to the local art gallery. Such is not my
intention. I merely wish to place before you
some considerations, I fear both obvious and
fragmentary, on that mysterious faculty by
which one should be able to derive an intelligent pleasure from the arts and letters, or, to
put it differently, the power to distinguish in
some measure what is real from what is false
in all that we read and see and hear.

There is no need for me to labour the importance of such a sense of discrimination.
There is no field of mental activity in which

the powers of discernment and judgment, of
criticism are not essential. In that vaguely
defined sphere of art such a capacity is not
easy to acquire. If we accept the division of
life in terms of a familiar formula, and look
on it as a search for *truth* or *goodness* or
beauty, we find that the last-named suggests
a quest with but little assistance from com-
pass and chart. The pursuit of truth in the
realm of natural science brings us, after all,
in touch with exact formulae as our guide.
In the laboratory or the observatory or in the
realm of pure mathematics we deal with things
that can be weighed and measured and reduced
to definite figures. In another domain, we are
led, most of us, by the beliefs and the code of
one accepted system of ethics or another,
shaped by the recorded experience of centuries. But in that vaguely-defined world of
what we call beauty we are, as it were, on
shifting sands. The canons of judgment seem
to be obscure. The scientist may say with
some finality, "that deduction is sound", or,
"this conclusion is false". Again, in the
sphere of morals we may judge our actions
by the code which we profess, but in the world
of the arts what is to be our guide? It seems
easier, at all events, to say what is scientific-
ally right or wrong, or what is morally good or

bad, than to say what is beautiful and what is not.

It is not a new question, this. It is, in fact, as old as civilization itself, but it has the freshness of a question which has never been fully answered and never will be. Life certainly would lose much interest for us if such an inquiry could meet the chilling finality of an ultimate reply. We are, of course, rather more apt to ask the question than were our ancestors. Our great-grandfathers here in North America cannot be said to have devoted a very large proportion of their time to the study of aesthetics. They had other things to do. But had they been men of leisure, they still, we may feel sure, would have looked upon beauty with some suspicion. I am indebted to a friend of mine for a quatrain which expresses our attitude—not the most sympathetic—towards their austere philosophy:

> The Puritan, as down life's path he goes,
> Gathers the thorn and casts away the rose,
> Thinking to please by this peculiar whim,
> The God who fashioned it and gave it him.

But there is, I think, little use in decrying the view of life held by our Puritan forbears. As a matter of fact the Puritan, in the first blush

of the reforming movement, did not set his
face against the beautiful. Cromwell's men
may have broken painted glass and sculptured
saint in their zeal, but Cromwell himself, as
we know, loved music. Be that as it may, the
more austere doctrines prevailed and for generations shaped the habits of the Anglo-Saxon
world on both sides of the Atlantic. Like all
philosophy, that of the Puritans was composed of virtues and the defects of those virtues, but in its heyday it had, at least, the
shining attribute of a remorseless sincerity.
We have, however, long since rejected their
strange legacy: the half-confessed idea that
ugliness is on the side of the angels—the belief, for example, that bright colours and grace
of line are slightly reprehensible.

A Puritan atmosphere lingered longer in
North America than in England. A simpler
life, relative poverty, and other causes kept
our physical surroundings, for instance, comparatively austere. The eighteenth century,
which to Europe meant elegance and urbanity,
not without a touch of cynicism, brushed this
continent but lightly. But the reaction to our
early dourness came later. We have still with
us monuments to that period when our architectural morals came to be sadly relaxed. It
was unfortunate that in the age which we

call "Victorian" we happened to become prosperous, because with the rejection of the simple ideas of an earlier period, so often beautiful in themselves, came that familiar passion for those architectural complications in which we rejoiced for their own sake.

These dark ages of taste happily belong to the past. We have emerged from that period of uncritical *parvenu* splendour. The superb architectural achievement of the post-war era—of which this country possesses fine examples in such profusion—is a comforting evidence of how far we have moved in the standards of public taste. As a matter of fact we have come to learn that beauty in our surroundings is not a fad, an isolated frippery or frill. The modern educationist, in particular, knows the importance of such things. The buildings in your modern colleges are a witness to the belief that physical environment is part of the equipment of education. If anyone doubts this let him study the manners of a group of schoolboys in some unlovely basement dining-room, and then place the same youths at their meals, let us say, in a dignified, well-proportioned hall, with lofty timbered roof and mullioned windows. Their manners will improve, and with their manners the point of view of which manners are a natural ex-

pression. We do well to recognize the fact
that the shape of our buildings affects the
shape of our minds, although this may seem
at times a somewhat disquieting thought.

Good taste, of course, is not always the
legacy of higher education. It is curious to
find, now and then, men of finely educated
mind with strange *lacunae* in their taste. I
remember visiting the home of a philosopher,
internationally distinguished, to discover on
his walls an oil painting of a village church,
in the tower of which the artist in a moment of
inspiration had placed a real and practicable
clock, with a mother-of-pearl face, which told
the time, and for all I know, struck the hours.
This *mariage de convenance* between beauty
and utility, however plausible in theory,
would, I think, be condemned by the most
liberal critic as unfortunate in practice. There
are many of the *cognoscenti* who may have a
respect for art and even some knowledge of it,
but who lack a feeling for it—which is, after
all, vastly different. A love of philosophic
truth is not inevitably accompanied by a sense
of beauty. Nor need a sense of beauty neces-
sarily reveal unerring taste. I am not thinking, at the moment, of those untempered
ecstasies evoked by flowers and sunsets, too
often committed to paper, combining a sensi-

tiveness to loveliness with crudely uncritical emotion. I refer to the lapse in taste of a real artist, such as a great architect, who will occasionally make the error of creating something of beauty out of relation to the purpose which it is meant to serve, or out of harmony with its surroundings. Perhaps he will lavish on a gymnasium the beauty more appropriate to a library or chapel. His feeling for beauty is impaired by a defective sense of proportion. Beauty and function cannot, of course, be unrelated. We would commend the judgment of anyone for passionately admiring such a thing of loveliness as Giotto's tower at Florence, but we would condemn the admirer if his admiration got so far out of hand as to lead him to duplicate it in some inappropriate place; and we might be tempted to homicide if he were to employ the replica for some practical use, let us say a reservoir or factory chimney. (For your peace of mind I may say I am suggesting an imaginary desecration.) Objects, however beautiful, must bear the right relation to the scheme of things as a whole. The modern poster, for instance, can be called a branch of art without straining the word, but however impressive may be these pictorial efforts to break down what the experts call our "sales-resistance", we rightly

murmur when they obscure for us the passing
vision of mountain and lake.

Beauty, like everything else, of course, is
best considered in relation to actual life. That
suggests one of the most satisfactory definitions of taste itself: a sense of beauty in relation to life. A piece of music can be studied
in the abstract, out of relation to our daily
existence; and so can painting—for modern
painting is often as abstract as music. But
when we come to beauty as applied to the
equipment of our physical environment we
are faced with considerations other than the
merely aesthetic. That attitude of mind which
lies behind what is called, politely, *art
moderne,* endeavours to house us in terms of
pure form and colour, possessing irrelevant
associations, with what result? Would I be
condemned for confessing that in an *art
moderne* dining-room my digestion is frankly
uneasy? A combination of cubes, circles and
triangles, in mauve and black and silver, may
demonstrate the canons of abstract beauty,
but I happen to prefer the more homely and
traditional appeal of Chippendale or Sheraton
or the brothers Adam. And why? There is
no question as to the charm of the colour and
line of the modernistic room considered
simply as a combination of line and colour,

but I fancy that most mortals are happier not
to conceive their environment entirely apart
from extraneous considerations. A Louis
XIV chair possesses graceful form, but we
like it not only for that but because of the
atmosphere of elegance and fine manners
which it conjures up. A Tudor window has
beauty in the pattern of its tracery and the
colour of its glass, but we like it too because
of that aroma of Elizabethan romance which
it suggests. We are, I suppose, most of us,
antiquarians or sentimentalists in such things.
Historical association has much to do with
our attitude towards the surroundings we
create. Applied art, therefore, it seems, does
well to pay some heed to tradition, just as it
must not neglect, of course, the obvious demands of efficiency which guide its creation.

Tradition and the necessities of function
must mould beauty to our needs, but that is,
after all, begging the question. What are the
canons of beauty? Who is to say what is bad
taste and what is good? Where is our ultimate authority? There is one famous experiment in official authority, as it happens, in the
realm of literature. The French Academy
stands guard over the French language with
jealous eye, and in such matters as the admission of words and their form, issues judg-

ments of taste from which there is no appeal.
But the French Academy operates in a society to which centralized direction is natural.
Anglo-Saxon ideas are less subject to govern-
ance and order. When our English language
is confronted with a slang phrase which has
gained increasing currency, it ultimately
swallows it, as an anaconda swallows a rabbit
—with an effort it is true, but with the consequence of an increased vitality. We have
numerous examples of self-constituted author-
ities on questions of taste to which we pay
elaborate deference. Modern journalism has
assumed a paternal attitude in such matters,
with the result that our standard of judgment in the applied arts, for instance, is
steadily improving. The improvement is
probably due, not so much to the final wisdom of the opinions offered as to the individual interest which is created by them.
There is no sphere in which man so yearns for
guidance as in the sphere of taste. That is
why most of us, in contemplating art, are
false to our natural Anglo-Saxon individualism. We carry on a pathetic search for
authority.

The court of public opinion is a natural
tribunal; but in the arts public opinion often
makes up in vehemence and prejudice what it

lacks in knowledge. The picture of a group of men and women in London solemnly subjecting an unpopular public statue to a coat of tar and feathers might suggest that our generation takes its art pretty seriously; but those good people were simply attempting to demonstrate their loyalty to what they conceived to be orthodoxy in the sculptor's art, and their action after all was negative. It would be more comforting to see the same amount of energy expended in raising money for another statue or for some equally constructive enterprise. The enemies of Mr. Epstein's "Rima" tarred and feathered her because they thought her too "futuristic"; but most of us, after all, are accustomed to deal just as ruthlessly with the past. We are ready to give an unequivocal and collective condemnation of an age to which we are successors, just as the Georgians united in decrying Gothic as a style of the barbarians. We are at present very rude, for instance, to the past century—rightly so most of us would say. There seems, in fact, little to be said in extenuation of that strange aesthetic aberration which passed over civilization in the 1870's and '80's. But our children will be interested to see how far a reaction in its favour will eventually come. Even now smart young persons are reviving horsehair furniture in their drawing-rooms. That is probably a sporadic fad. But the despised waxflowers have returned, possibly to stay. Will Victorianism as a cult some day be resuscitated? Shall we have a return of antimacassars and china dogs and whatnots and stuffed owls and cast iron deer? Who knows?

We live, as we know—and often say—in a mechanical age when most of life, including almost art itself, seems standardized. But in our attitude toward art, in other words in the sphere of taste, we should be able to find one happy means of escape from this all-pervading mechanization of life. No two minds, if they function honestly, will reveal quite the same reaction to a given stimulus. If we are true to ourselves each of us will follow, as far as we are permitted, his own or her own law in this matter of taste. A character in a novel of Mr. E. V. Lucas asked that his only epitaph should be the two words, "He discriminated". Perhaps it sounds a bit snobbish, at first blush, this boast of having distinguished between the right things and the wrong things—almost as if one was proud to have chosen the right people as companions rather than the wrong ones. But that is an unfair construction. After all,

there should not be anything improper or unusual about such an attitude. It is surely
the duty of educated men and women to exercise their critical faculty wisely and courage-
ously. One of the major tasks performed by
the college is surely to give its spiritual off-
spring first the desire, and secondly the
capacity to know the difference between the
genuine and the meretricious in what they
see about them; to distinguish real feeling
from sentimentality, the noble from the
merely florid, the tragic from the sordid, the
dramatic from the theatrical.

How are we to acquire such a critical sense?
Not by any superficial means. We cannot
learn the principles of beauty by taking
courses in interior decoration or lectures in
musical appreciation, necessary as such things
are in their proper place. To learn fundamentals one must go back to fundamental
sources. In discussing the education of taste
in literature, Sir Richard Jebb once gave his
view as to how this was to be accomplished:

> Classical studies", so he says, "help to preserve
> sound standards of literature. It is not difficult to
> lose such standards . . . It is peculiarly easy to do
> so in days when the lighter and more ephemeral
> kinds of writing form for many people the staple
> of daily reading. The fashions of the hour may

start a movement not in the best direction, which
may go on until the path is difficult to retrace. The
humanities, if they cannot prevent such a movement, can do something to temper and counteract
it; because they appeal to permanent things, to the
instinct for beauty in human nature, and to
the emotions, and in any one who is at all sus-
ceptible to their influence, they develop a literary
conscience.

What is true of literature is true of the arts.
Taste is not inherited nor can it be purchased,
nor is it to be acquired in polite conversation.
Our critical judgment and capacity to understand fine things can be trained only by a
familiarity with fine things. I wish we had
fewer textbooks about pictures and music and
poetry, and a closer acquaintance with the
things themselves, which in an age of perfect
mechanical reproduction no longer presents a
difficulty. Most collectors of pictures or snuff-
boxes or old silver or prints will confess that
their judgment grew with their collection,
that only by living with their purchases could
they learn to distinguish the bad from the
good and the good from the second-best. The
lover of old furniture appraises a fine piece
through some sixth sense—no rule of thumb
will help him, no textbook on "periods" or
makers will greatly assist. The textbook mind

is, of course, one of the perils of our age—
the mind which asks for an answer to the
questions of life in Section B of Chapter 2 of
Prof. X's handbook. Beware the textbook
mind! We do not escape the danger when we
leave college. Everywhere we are confronted
by that depressing efficiency which supplies us
with elaborate tabulations of second-hand
ideas. The modern printing-press sometimes
seems to have abrogated its duty of stimulat-
ing thought in order to address itself to the
task of making thought unnecessary. It is in
college, of course, that we are privileged to
acquire the value of independent thinking. I
am grateful for a wholesome shock I received
as an undergraduate. I had made some observation in an essay on mediaeval history
which interested my tutor, who asked me my
authority for the opinion. I quoted the
name of a historian, respectable and learned,
whose opinions were impressive. "Did you
consult any original documents?" asked my
tutor. I replied in the negative. "Humph,"
he grunted, "you'll be finding your ideas in
the newspapers next." But this is a digression. If our sense of discernment is improved
by association with objects of beauty, there
might seem to be some educational value to
be found in contact with things at the other

end of the aesthetic scale. The public in European cities is occasionally subjected to what are called "atrocity exhibitions"—collections of objects supposed to sin against the more obvious standards of taste. It is possibly a useful piece of popular education to show us occasionally "how not to do it", but what a threat to domestic peace and harmony must lurk in such an exhibition! And what a shock too to find placed on view by unfeeling hands, to be gazed at by a callous public, some half-forgotten treasure of our youthful mind!

How is the college to help us to acquire a critical faculty? Some intimacy with fine literature and the arts is somehow not sufficient in itself. We have consciously to develop a definite sense of criticism. I need not say that I am not using criticism in the false sense in which it is often loosely used. I suppose the fact that we often think of the critic in terms of disparagement is an evidence of our failure to understand his function. Criticism is, of course, not depreciation, still less is it to be associated with eulogy. It means a full understanding through the process of examination. Lord Morley, in a fine passage, speaks of the

. . . synthetic criticism, which, after analysis has done its work, and disclosed to us the peculiar qualities of form, conception, and treatment, shall collect the products of this first process, construct for us the poet's mental figure in its integrity and just coherence, and then finally, as the sum of its work, shall trace the relations of the poet's ideas, either direct or indirect, through the central currents of thought, to the visible tendencies of an existing age.

The critic, after all, is not a mere minor accessory to the artist. Disraeli was the author of a jibe as untrue as it was cruel when he said "the critics were the men who failed". Criticism in its real sense, as we of course know, is to be recognized as one of the highest forms of intellectual activity. As a recent author has put it, "Taste—critical judgment, discernment—is the most delicate fruit of learning and grows at the top of the tree". It would appear, however, that this critical faculty usually develops in a community only after some achievement in the arts has first taken place. As in so many things, we seem to generate power before we acquire the ability to control and guide it.

The critical mind for the student to cultivate is one which takes nothing for granted, which will accept no opinion on another's authority, which arrives at no conclusion without independent thought. The educated mind forms its own conclusions and is able to defend them. We are all familiar with the time-honoured and melancholy observation, "I know nothing about art but I know what I like". With the first part of the comment we may be generally in complete agreement as representing an accurate statement, but what about the second clause? If we know nothing about art *do* we really know what we like? Are we entitled to any preferences if we are unable to explain why we possess them? Is there a form of conscious training which can help us? I recently came across an interesting experiment in education in taste through the medium of poetry. A professor at an English university has made a practice of asking his students to make comments on passages of verse as a mental exercise, without knowledge of either their authors or titles. The results, to judge from a recently published reference to them, were illuminating. One undergraduate, in making a comment on Hardy's poem written on the death of Meredith, observed magnificiently,

This might have been written by one commonplace clergyman of another commonplace clergyman.

Another critic-in-the-making apparently decided that this poem was

> The work of someone who, whilst acquainted with
> much at second-hand, has not taken the trouble
> to acquire his own set of experiences as a basis for
> values and judgment.

Many of the young ladies and gentlemen apparently looked on the extracts placed before
them less as a reflection of the poet's mind
than as a text for the expression of their own
emotional reactions to life. But nevertheless
such an experiment seems worth while so long
as it results in creating an increased sensitive-
ness to the stimulus to be found in literature,
or in giving the student an awareness of what
lies within books.

However we acquire it, our equipment for
life should include what might be called an
aesthetic conscience. This conscience must be
sensitive, but it will do to be rational as well.
There is to be preserved a delicate balance
between intellect and emotion. We cannot
appreciate music, for instance, with the mind
alone. Few of us can honestly emulate the
concert-goer who follows the score of musical
composition. Through such a practice one
seems to be approaching music through the
intellect alone. Leibnitz offered a provocative

definition of music when he called it "arithmetic made self-conscious". Music, of course, has a mathematical structure which has a beauty of its own, but its primary appeal is surely to the senses, and those of us who enjoy it as an emotional experience, however uninstructed we may be, are not outside the pale of those for whom its delights were intended. And so with all art. It is possible to over-intellectualize it but, on the other hand, if we apply emotion untempered by intelligence, the result is worse—the sin of sentimentality. I hope I am not disturbing any psychological orthodoxy when I suggest again that the appeal of the arts must be jointly to mind and senses.

Our senses might well seem to run the risk of being dulled by over-stimulus in an age of twenty-four foot posters and electric signs and cacophony in many forms—both deliberate and accidental. It is probable that we shall learn some day that mere noise is not emphasis, and that over-statement in art as well as in language ultimately defeats its own purpose. Until such a golden age of restraint is reached an effort is required to keep our aesthetic conscience from becoming too seared to be open to the subtler influences which so often possess the most significance.

Our aesthetic conscience must, of course, be many-sided. The sense of sight might seem to be more highly developed than the others until we come to realize the daily scenes with which most of us human beings seem to be contented. Again, as our hearing is further trained and sensitized I wonder what changes will come, for instance, in our musical programmes, often as ill-chosen as they are well performed. And if improvement might come in our programmes of music, what moderation can and will be effected in those sounds in modern life which are not music? And there are other fields to be cultivated. Even the lowly sense of taste itself is not unworthy of our attention. Perhaps the science of dietetics when it considers aesthetics as part of its duty—but I must avoid dangerous ground!

The appreciation of art in all its forms, abstract and applied, is abundantly worthy of the attention of the university mind. Art is too often thought of only in relation to sonnets, symphonies and old masters, but the same principles are to be found in the streets and rooms we have to see hourly, and in the tools of our everyday life. The concepts underlying a treatise on aesthetics are, after all, no different from those governing the design of a lampshade. The restriction of our sense of criticism to an occasional concert or art exhibition and the fleeting hour we grudgingly give to real literature, may well remind us of that kind of religion which is reserved for Sunday alone. Most human beings must find their aesthetic stimulus chiefly on the hoarding and in the newspaper or on the walls of whatever may be their home. We are influenced, after all, by what we see oftenest. This suggests to the trained aesthetic conscience its opportunity and its appropriate task. In a famous passage Milton says:

> I cannot praise a fugitive and cloistered virtue, unexercised and unbreathed, that never sallies out and seeks her adversary . . .

You will remember how it runs. This was written, of course, in terms of a moral issue. If we apply it to the world of art—the fine arts and the applied arts as well—it teaches its own lesson. If the university mind, sensitive to beauty and as discerning as sensitive, and above all possessed of a public spirit, which rejects the seclusion of cloistered beauty and sallies out to seek the adversaries, philistinism and ugliness and sentimentality remaining about us, there is no telling what victories it might still achieve.

STEEL IN THE MODERN WORLD

*At the Annual Convention of the
American Institute of Steel Construction, Biloxi, Mississippi,
14th November, 1929*

Mr. Chairman and Gentlemen:

I am very happy that it was possible to fore-
gather with the members of the American Institute of Steel Construction on this most interesting occasion. Your invitation to Canada's representative at Washington is a very
pleasant compliment to Canada.

I notice, Mr. Chairman, that you have as-
signed to me the subject of international co-
operation. It is natural to do so because that,
of course, is the object of the diplomat's trade.
International co-operation is the task of diplomacy just as building in steel is the concern
of your institute. I don't want, however, to
take up your time this evening by talking
about the technicalities of the diplomat's
work, still less do I wish to offer any profound
observations on the science of metallurgy or
on the profession of engineering. There are,
however, some points in common between your

job and my job which might be interesting to
explore.

It might be said that the vocabulary of your
profession and mine have much in common.
I pass over one alleged point of similarity.
You are interested in the fabrication of steel,
but you are not alone in this undertaking, if
we are to believe the unkind things which have
been said about the diplomat's alleged love
of fabrication. Then there is another process
in the technique of steel manufacture which
seems to have a bearing on one tendency of
modern diplomacy. The diplomat is now so
given to making speeches that one is naturally
reminded of the hot air blast which I believe
represents one stage in the manufacture of
steel. However, you, as makers of great
structures are naturally familiar with the
problem of wind resistance. I notice that you
even have a committee on wind-bracing. Perhaps that was set up in anticipation of your
visitor's address. I shall certainly endeavour
to profit from one lesson which you have to
teach—just as a steel girder has a definite limitation of length and a recognized point at
which the breaking strain is reached, so must
a speech in the hands of a speaker with any
conscience also have a limitation of length,
and the audience a definite breaking strain of
endurance.

Well, gentlemen, I have suggested that steel has a bearing on international life. It could not be said that its first appearance was in the interests of harmony, for we first find it as applied to the manufacture of swords and breast-plates, long before it was used for ploughshares or pruning-hooks. If we turn, however, to the world of to-day and think of the function of steel in international affairs, communication and transportation come naturally to our minds. There is no form of inter-communication which does not depend on some contribution from this metal. And so here in North America our two nations are sewn together physically by threads of steel, not only by the railway lines and motor cars which cross our common border but by the great bridges which span our international waterways. These, of course, have a direct relation to the functions of your organization, which is concerned directly with the problems of structural steel. That graceful structure known as the Peace Bridge, between Buffalo and Fort Erie, was opened two years ago with an impressive ceremonial, not only as a fine achievement of the engineer and architect but as a practical monument to good relations between the nations which it physically joined. Three days ago another bridge, the Ambassador Bridge between Detroit and Windsor, was formally opened. It is a striking evidence of the inter-communication between the United States and Canada that twenty millions of dollars should be spent on this structure. The skill of the engineer has achieved a new record in this undertaking, for the 1,850 foot suspension span of this bridge is, so I understand, the longest in the world. There are frontiers less civilized than ours where greater amounts are spent and more steel manufactured for the purpose, not of letting people in but of keeping them out.

The modern development of steel, like most scientific achievements, has a long and distinguished international pedigree. All the great countries of the world have made their contribution to the creation of this commodity in its present form. It is not for me to discourse on a subject which you know so well; but a layman finds, with intense interest, how many nations have contributed to the perfection of a material to which society is so much indebted. We owe, I believe, the perfection of the open hearth process in its highest form to the Swedes; in Spain the use of a water blast made possible a higher temperature in smelting than was possible before; in Germany the height of furnaces was increased and their shape altered to provide for a greater volume of metal; England first used coal instead of charcoal, for smelting on a commercial basis. No invention would be complete—at least it would not be safe to say it was complete—without giving some credit to Scotland, and it was Scottish genius which replaced the old leather bellows in smelting by the invention of an air-pump. A French inventor learned how to utilize furnace gases which hitherto had been wasted, and the English Sir Henry Bessemer introduced the modern era of steel manufacture by processes which it would be an impertinence for me to describe, even if I could. Your own great national accomplishments in this field need no comment from me.

The membership of your institute is itself an example of international co-operation. I am glad to know that business men from Canada are assuming their share of the significant work you are doing. Your joint efforts lead not only to the advancement of the industry of structural steel, which is your immediate objective, but you serve a wider purpose still in promoting material progress generally by extending the use of steel construction. I congratulate you on the tasks which you undertake to perform. Mechanical efficiency is served by your work in standardization; the margin of safety in our modern cities is widened by the codes of practice which you impose; and numerous and invaluable economies are effected by your researches into structural methods.

As I have already said, the physical progress of society is quickened by what is done to widen the use of steel. It seems almost self-evident that prosperity in a material sense can almost be measured by the yardstick of steel. If this be true, then I can point without hesitation to the progress which is to be seen in all sections of my own country, and I offer as a significant evidence of the advance which we are making in Canada the fact that we are producing and using more structural steel. According to the latest annual estimate, that of last year, the tonnage of fabricated steel shapes for construction purposes increased by fully one-half over the output of the previous year. The capital invested in this branch of industry rose about one-seventh during the twelve months, and the value of the production was greater by one-quarter than that of the previous record year.

We are, of course, in a very happy position in Canada. No civilized country is as fortunate as we are in the possession of vast

undeveloped riches. Those of you who have
been in the Dominion during the last few
years will realize to what extent we are rolling
back the curtains which hitherto have hidden
the possibilities of our great north. In fact,
we are busy discovering ourselves in Canada.
An instance of this occurred not long ago. I
remember one fact which impressed itself on
my memory as a schoolboy studying geography—that however rich my own province
of Ontario was in most things, it had no coal.
A few weeks ago a deposit of lignite coal some
two square miles in extent was found within
sixty miles of the Hudson Bay. The discovery of these 20,000,000 tons is an example
of what is happening in the northern districts
of six of our provinces. The figures covering
mineral products in all forms reveal a constant increase. It is, therefore, not surpris-
ing that, in the metallic mining industries
alone, in five years the figures representing
capital and men employed and the net value of
product have doubled.

The conquest of nature can only be accomplished with the aid of science. The members of your institute are quick to appreciate
the value of research in industry. The government of Canada have set up a body under a
distinguished head to carry on such a service,

which represents a co-ordination of scientist,
industrialist and public servant in the work
of developing our natural resources and manufacturing their product. Imposing buildings
will soon rise above the Ottawa River to house
this important activity. A research foundation under the government of Ontario is also
playing an important part in this war against
nature on our northern frontiers. Steel
manufacturers will be interested in their
efforts to bring into commercial use the great
deposits of iron ore which exist in Ontario
and which are, possibly, an extension of the
iron ranges of Minnesota.

Well, gentlemen, I could, if my conscience
would let me, give you plenty of figures to
show our development. But statistics, like
children, are better seen than heard. Let me
mention just one activity of special interest
to you. A very sure index of prosperity and
confidence is to be found in the figures of
construction. Last year's industrial construction represented an investment 58 per cent.
greater than the year before, and in the last
seven years the figures covering general building contracts have nearly doubled. You may
be interested to know that we have become
skyscraper addicts in Canada and now in my
own city of Toronto, to show it, we are erect-

ing the tallest building in the British Empire.
The skyscraper, after all, is not a bad expression of material advancement in itself. It
represents in one unit the research of the
metallurgist, the daring of the engineer and
the imagination of the architect. The critic
may, of course, object that it belongs to an
age that has robbed life of much of its charm
and beauty. I heard a story the other day
of an English visitor who was being shown
about the streets of an enterprising city, not,
as a matter of fact, unconnected with the steel
industry. His guide pointed with pride to a
street of tall buildings and told him how many
dozen skyscrapers the community possessed.
"A good thing," said the visitor, as he looked
up at the murky heavens, "your sky does
need scraping."

It is striking to realize how short a time
ago this type of structure was developed. As
you know, it was not until about 1880 that
structural iron was thought of as a commercial
possibility for the erection of buildings. We
have apparently to thank the pressure of insurance rates for the development of metal
as a building material. A great fire in New
York, so we find, led builders to think of fireproof construction. Enterprising architects
commenced to put up structures with iron

columns to reduce the fire hazard. And then a daring genius in the early 'eighties designed a building for an insurance company in Chicago, rising to the dizzy height of ten storeys, with a metal frame to carry the weight of the walls. At that moment the modern skyscraper had its birth. It is easy to forget that a limitation in height was, however, imposed on the building until electricity was employed for lighting and for the motive power of elevators. Then the skyscraper was finally released and a great impetus skyward was given it.

May I congratulate you sincerely on one branch of your activities in which I believe you are making progress. I refer to your efforts to control that light-hearted disturber of our peace, the riveter. Solomon was, we are given to believe, a very wise man, but he was never so wise as when he contrived to build his temple without noise. I am told that welding can now be a substitution for riveting on all joints except where the greatest stresses are found. May we hope—if I am not entering upon the field of technical controversy—that with your enterprise and inventiveness, the welder may ultimately rout the riveter completely, and that one element at least may be removed from the gehenna of noise in which most of us have to live.

There is no doubt about the efficiency of
steel construction. What, one may ask, has it
done for the appearance of our cities? A
distinguished Englishman was once shown one
of the early steel buildings in New York. His
guide boasted to him that it was absolutely
fireproof, that whatever happened, it simply
could not burn. After a moment's pause the
only comment was, "What a pity". But that
remark would be entirely unfair to the skyscraper of to-day. The form of the modern
towered building, with its recesses and set-
backs and graceful apex, which has been
created by the genius of your architects, working within the limits of city building laws, has
given us a thing of gracefulness and charm.
As a matter of fact I always object on principle to the view that beauty and efficiency are
generally to be found on opposite sides of the
fence. If a thing does its job well, if it is
really efficient in the big sense of the word, the
probability is that it will be good to look at.
Modern bridge construction shows, I suppose,
an enormous improvement in the economy of
material, simplicity and speed of construction,
and, in most cases, engineering necessities are
thought of before decorative detail, but the
result is that nowadays one very rarely sees
an ugly bridge.

Whatever one may think of the relation of steel to the appearance of modern cities, there is no question that the first application of iron to building was none too happy in its effect. This, of course, was largely because the builders of the day did not know how to use this new building material. I do not suppose we have any survivals of those buildings of a certain period which rejoiced in a cast iron front, a metal skin of iron actually anchored to the brickwork of a building. Those were the days when iron had a sudden vogue. We can remember the cast iron dogs and deer which dotted the lawns of the day, and the cast iron boys in fountains holding a cast iron umbrella. We almost had cast iron rain as well!

John Ruskin, with characteristic assurance, once expressed certain opinions about the use of iron in building. It is amusing to look down Broadway to-day and to think of the rules this great critic of architecture promulgated not more than fifty years ago:

> The rule is . . . that metals may be used as a *cement* but not as a *support* . . . the moment that the iron in the least degree takes the place of the stone and acts by its resistance to crushing and bears superincumbent weight, . . . or if, in the form of a rod or girder, it is used to do what wooden beams

would have done as well, that instant the building ceases, so far as such applications of metal extend, to be true architecture.

Ruskin was even prepared to offer an opinion on the metallurgical side of iron construction. "No builder," he warned the profession in 1880, "has true command over the changes in the crystalline structure of iron or its modes of decay." Mr. Ruskin, however, was, as often happened, proved wrong and it is due to the modern manufacturer, with the quiet work of the scientist behind him, that the builder now knows just what he may expect of the steel which he uses, without the risk of error.

If Ruskin were alive to-day, it would, no doubt, be possible to demonstrate to his satisfaction that skyscrapers will not fall down. It might be more difficult to convince him of their beauty. Most of us, however, do not require conversion on either score. There is a fascination to be found in the modern towered building which is irresistible. This is not only because of its structural scheme or because of its lines. There is more in it than that. We have something in us which responds to the work of the builder. An achievement in construction represented by sixty or eighty storeys makes its own appeal. No crowd in a busy street is too busy to watch a steam-shovel at work below, or a great girder swinging into place above. Is this interest in building the same as that which expresses itself in wooden blocks on the nursery floor? The psychologist may, of course, tell us that the destructive impulse in us is as strong as our desire to build. He may remind us how we took the clock to pieces in our infancy, and may suggest that we watch the fall of a factory chimney with even more zest than its construction. Perhaps we do, but I propose to go on believing that the work of construction and creation makes the more profound appeal. For this reason, and for many others, we are grateful to such a great organization as yours which has lent increased precision and widened scope to the science and the art of building.

THE MOTOR CAR AS AMBASSADOR

*At the Annual Convention of the
American Automobile Association, Washington, 19th March,
1930*

Mr. Chairman and Gentlemen:

I am very glad to have the privilege, to-day, of meeting the custodians of those mystical letters, the three A's, which mean so much to the motoring community of this great country. I am almost awestruck by the power which is wielded by the vast organizations represented here in this room. You had, I am told, in the United States in 1928, one motor to every five persons. Therefore, with a little crowding, perhaps, on the back seat, the entire population in this country could take a drive at the same time. It is an amazing accomplishment to be achieved in less than a single generation.

The motor car has, of course, become an essential and indispensable part of the mechanism of society. I am not sure that we yet know how to use it as wisely as we might, for either pleasure or profit, but here it is at our service, its usefulness widening every year.

The American Automobile Association and
organizations like it throughout the world
have done much to bring about this result. It
is, after all, only two or three decades ago
when some of us were nodding our heads with
grave misgivings over the demoralization of
home life which the motor car seemed certain
to bring about. Occasionally we were told
of irate citizens in the country districts who
took on themselves the salvation of society by
sprinkling tacks on the road in the path of
these monsters from the city. Those days
seem far away and, thanks to the educational
services of bodies like yours, and the movement for good roads which you have so ably
promoted, the motor car has become so necessary a servant of man—so essential a piece of
modern mechanism—that the material structure of civilization would almost collapse without it.

As in most countries, the automobile has
made very striking headway in Canada in the
last few years. In the decade following the
Great War, the number of cars registered in
the Dominion increased fourfold and, I may
say, the opportunities of the automobile are
increasing equally, for in the last seven years
the mileage of surfaced roads has lengthened
by almost a third. The motor car has an

especially important mission to perform in a country like ours, where distances are so great and our population so scattered. But this, of course, applies to many lands. In fact, it is worth while to stop and think now and then just what a far-reaching effect on life everywhere the automobile has brought about. If we look for a single mechanical device comparable to it in its importance we should have to search many centuries. It has, for example, created a revolution in the economic world. But this, however, is no place to discuss the effect of motor transport on agricultural prices, or the extension of urban areas, or the opening up and development of regions which without the motor would be inaccessible.

Perhaps its effects on social life are even greater. We have not begun to see the consequences of the contact between town and country which the motor car makes possible. It has an important bearing on the health of both. Through its agency the amenities of the city are thrown open to the country dweller, and the greater charms of country life are brought within reach of those who live in the towns. I say "greater charms", because I confess my sympathies are often on the side of the country as against the city. You may know the story of the English countryman who was asked if he never wanted to go to London to see the sights? "No, zurr," he said, looking contemptuously at a motor full of city folk, "no, zurr, they comes down to see us."

Important as these functions are, to-day I cannot help thinking rather of another service performed by the motor in serving as an international link. No two countries can be so conscious of this particular function as the United States and Canada. We have a perpetual demonstration before our eyes of the extent to which the motor can give to two neighbouring peoples a knowledge of each other. Last year over four and a half million United States cars entered the Dominion of Canada, one-half as many automobiles as we have people in the Dominion. During the months of July and August an observer sitting beside one of our highways can make a very satisfactory study of United States geography by a scrutiny of the licence plates on the passing cars. But this is not a one-way visitation. In the same year—last year—we sent you over six hundred thousand Canadian motors. I should like to draw your attention to the fact that the movement south was *relatively* greater than the movement north. To come up to our standard as visiting neighbours, in proportion to population, I must politely point out that you will have to send us seven and a half million cars. You will see, therefore, what a large leeway you have still to make up in order to achieve parity—in visits.

Travel, of course, has not only an international aspect, it has important national implications as well. If it makes neighbouring people see each other's point of view more clearly, it serves to strengthen the national traditions on each side of a common boundary. The visitor to a foreign land, after all, goes there to see things which he cannot find at home. He seeks a foreign atmosphere. He wants to see the historical monuments, the national shrines, the birthplaces of famous men, the great battle-fields which are part and parcel of the history of the nation he is visiting. For instance, when we visit this great country we take especial pleasure in making a pilgrimage to Mount Vernon to enjoy its eighteenth-century beauty and the spell of history which pervades the old estate. We want to see the first structures you reared in the cause of education in New England or in Virginia. We like to view the field of Gettysburg, with the great story which is mingled with its soil. We delight in studying those springs of your national life which are sym-

bolized by what we find in such places as Salem
and Jamestown and Charleston and Valley
Forge. Similarly, when you visit Canada, we
find that what you want to see there are such
things as the ancient citadel of Halifax, the
remains of the early settlements at Annapolis
Royal or the old colonial city of Fredericton,
the grey ramparts of Quebec, so weighted with
history, or those structures which mark the
foundations of life in Upper Canada at Kings-
ton and Toronto and Queenston Heights, or
the monuments to pioneering in our Western
provinces.

In Canada, of course, you will find interesting contrasts between the old and new. I
needn't remind you that often in a setting old
and picturesque, we can show you industry
in its most modern form. In the ancient province of Quebec it is still possible, for example,
some of my lawyer friends tell me, to find
amongst the title deeds of an old farm, a document bearing the sign manual of King Louis
XIV himself as the original grantor of the
land; and yet in this old civilization, with its
beautiful seventeenth-century churches and its
thatched barns, there are some of the most
progressive modern developments to be found
in the generation of water power and the
manufacture of paper. In the west of Canada

are still visible the ruins of such fortifications as were left by the Hudson's Bay Company, with its two hundred and fifty years of history. But above these ancient remains of pioneering days can now be heard the whirr of the modern aeroplane, engaged in transportation or in patrolling the forest against the menace of fire. Again, at Churchill, on the shores of Hudson Bay, where the remains of Fort Prince of Wales have for generations seen no life but the seagulls, the engineer is now busy restoring an old and abandoned seventeenth-century harbour to new uses as a great ocean port. And so on, in countless places, there is a dramatic contrast between youth and age. We have the centuries of that British tradition which we have inherited and cherish. But on the other hand, we are one of the few countries which still has a new frontier on our north, where the pioneer still lives and labours. This is one of the things which give Canada its characteristic atmosphere of which the visitor is aware and of which he often reminds the resident.

And so this growing habit of touring—"tourism"—serves this double purpose of spreading international friendliness on the one hand, and on the other, of deepening the appreciation of those characteristics which lie

at the base of real nationality, rightly understood. These, after all, are the differences
which save the world from the monotony of
sameness. The better we are educated to know
the meaning of these varying national traditions and appreciate them and understand
them, the better it will be for the world as a
whole. We should be grateful, therefore, for
the aid to be found in such organizations as
yours, for it is perhaps not too extravagant to
think of the motor cars in their summer voyag-
ing like so many million shuttles moving back-
ward and forward over frontiers throughout
the world, helping to weave across these seams
a fabric of understanding.

FAREWELL SPEECH

*At a Farewell Dinner Given by
the Pilgrims of the United
States, New York, 4th .June,
1930.*

Mr. President and Gentlemen:

It is very difficult, indeed, gentlemen, for me
to express myself on this occasion with any
degree of adequacy. You have done me an
honour, this evening, which I appreciate more
sincerely than I can say. Three years ago,
last February, you gave me, as a new and
green diplomat, a warm and generous welcome
which I shall never forget. Now, when I take
my departure after this sojourn in your midst,
the generous words which have been spoken
touch me very deeply indeed.

I need not say that I have felt it a very
great honour to serve as the first Minister
which my country has sent to yours. The
mutual knowledge existing between the
United States and Canada commenced, of
course, many generations ago, and the intercourse between us is growing in intensity and
volume yearly; but, until 1927, we never, as

it were, spoke directly to each other. To have been one of the instruments, along with your distinguished Minister, Mr. Phillips, in opening up this new communication, has been a privilege which I find difficult to describe.

My work in Washington has been made peculiarly enjoyable by the kindness and friendliness of that most warmhearted of communities. I cannot begin to say how deeply I appreciate the generous co-operation which I have received from the two Secretaries of State whom I have had the honour to know, Mr. Kellogg and Mr. Stimson. I have been singularly fortunate, too, in my colleagues at the British Embassy. Sir Esme Howard's great gift for friendship requires no description to this audience, and the spirit of comradeship which he and every member of his staff have invariably shown is no less present in his distinguished successor. I am very happy indeed to have had the privilege of serving as Sir Ronald Lindsay's colleague, if only for a few months. But time will not permit me to say more of those both in public and private life who have contributed so much to the pleasure of the task of organizing our new legation.

Since I came to Washington, my wife and I have endeavoured to see as much of the life

of the United States as the activities at your
capital permitted. I might say, sir, that we
hoped to see something of every one of your
states before leaving. Time and space, however, have so conspired against us that we
shall take our leave having visited, I am
afraid, only thirty-two—just two-thirds of the
total. But I am very happy to feel that we have
travelled through as much of your country
as we have. The diplomat who endeavours
to see the United States of America through
the spectacles of New York and Washington
is attempting an impossible task. I hasten to
say, sir, that I am casting no reflection on the
spectacles—I am simply pointing out the
magnitude of the view. As one moves through
this vast country, as we have done, whenever
this has been possible, and have seen those differences which mark the background and life
of the various regions in north, south, east
and west, one is conscious that your Republic
is really composed of many nations, each with
its own history and charm and its individual
outlook. But through the pattern of your
national tapestry, diversified as it may be,
there runs one golden thread of warmth and
hospitality to the visitor.

On an occasion like this, I think we must
accept certain references to our mutual

boundary as inevitable. The cynic may say
that the customary observations are but platitudes, and that even an epigram on the subject
is no better because an epigram is, after all,
as some one has said, only "a platitude on its
night out". But, however obvious it may
seem, we should never be ashamed of remind-
ing ourselves of the truth, which is illustrated
by the traditions of what is, after all, the most
civilized frontier in the world.

It is, of course, inevitable that questions
should occasionally arise between us which
might tend to misunderstanding. It would
not be the part of candour to overlook them.
The open recognition of such problems is the
first step towards their solution. The issues
which now and then disturb us, as a matter
of fact, are the product of our very intimacy
and the intricacy of our relations. But what
may ruffle the surface need not stir the depths.
We now have the tradition of one hundred and
fifteen years of peace between us, based on
self-control and common sense. I witnessed
a graphic illustration of this—the sort of re-
presentation of a truth which pageantry can
often give us—two and a half years ago, when
President Coolidge very graciously received
a detachment of Canadian troops which had
come to Washington to take part in a cere-

mony. As I was waiting at the White House
for the President I noticed on the wall of the
drawing-room a portrait of General Washington, with an inscription attached to the frame,
to the effect that the picture had been saved
from the fire of 1814 by Mrs. Madison. I re-
called the occasion of this conflagration, of
which I shall not remind you. At the same
moment my eye fell on the scarlet tunics and
white helmets of the troops drawn up on the
lawn—the first British soldiers under arms
to come to Washington since then—this time
on a very different mission. The stretch of
time—one hundred and thirteen years—was
made dramatic, for in that century and more,
the peace which was formally realized in 1815
has been, to borrow the terminology of war,
"not only won but consolidated".

We have learned to know and understand
each other. We can appreciate each other's
point of view and the reasons which lie behind
it. If we find the workings of each other's
constitution occasionally difficult to compre-
hend, we know what is more important, the
human beings who work under them. We are
even capable of understanding each other's
jokes, and that, as some one has wisely said,
is the ultimate test of mutual understanding.
It is not an extravagance to say that we have

erected personal contact into a principle of
international relations. No mutual knowledge can come about without it. M. Jusserand
says in one of his essays:

> Experience has already shown and will more and
> more show that no invention, no telephone, no aero-
> plane, no wireless will ever replace the knowledge
> of a country and the understanding of a people's
> dispositions.

To depend on science, however ingenious
the invention, as a means of international contact, can only lead to disappointment. The
importance of the human factor is increasing.

This has its application, of course, to the
wider group which, for want of a more accurate term, we call "the English-speaking
world". Here we stand in need of increased
personal intercourse. It may sound like a
truism to say so, but it is surely difficult to
over-estimate the importance of personal contact between the American and British
peoples. I am not thinking only of the annual migrations which, through the ease of
modern touring, are happily increasing. (I
am not thinking *at all* of the exuberant young
men who spend a meteoric fortnight in a
foreign country and produce a self-confident
volume as a result.) What I mean to say is

that the world stands in especial need of the
interchange of visits between those whose public responsibilities give them both meaning
and consequence. There is nothing, surely,
in the international sphere which will so re-
pay the efforts of public men as this. One can
almost regard such intercourse as being the
practice of peace as distinguished from the
theory.

One can say with no suspicion of rhetoric
that the relations existing between the two
great branches of the English-speaking world
are on a truer and sounder basis now than they
have been for many years. One is conscious
of a deepened friendship, of a strengthened
mutual comprehension between them. It is
marked by no formal alliance; that we readily
reject as inappropriate. There is, after all,
nowhere a greater dislike of the written word,
in matters of statecraft, than in an Empire
like ours, which has never accepted even the
idea of its constitution being committed to
paper. There is not even a formal *entente*
between us. An understanding—yes—but we
use that simple word with no technical meaning. The sort of understanding we believe in
is that which comes when each says to the
other: "What are your difficulties? Here are
mine."

There is no reason why understanding between us should lead to misunderstanding elsewhere. We believe that friendship, far from being an exclusive thing, is actually contagious. The Anglo-Saxon (or Anglo-Celt, if it is safer to use that term) is not given to racialism; he is not given to propaganda—he does not understand it. Most of us in the British-American world may speak English, but we do not speak it in the spirit of the Scots parson, who was asked by one of his parishioners why he always said his prayers in Gaelic (The rest of the service was in English, and this seemed to be an inexplicable exception.) The old man answered: "Ah, laddie, I dinna like to approach the Almighty in a translation."

There is, of course, a community of feeling between our peoples which can be taken for granted. Your people, when they come to Canada to stay, become British subjects as a matter of course. Canadians similarly, as residents here, accept your citizenship. There is something significant in the fact that Americans and Englishmen who are resident in each other's country are rapidly assimilated in the population, and it is striking that the new citizenship, however loyally interpreted, is not looked upon as incompatible with a

sentimental regard for the old allegiance.
Americans in Great Britain and Englishmen
in the United States are the best exponents of
the true harmony which should exist between
the patriotic feeling of the good citizen and
the generous attitude of the good neighbour.

There is a story of a patron of art who
bought an old master in Italy and in order,
let us say, to comply with the niceties of the
customs regulations for purposes of importation, had a landscape temporarily painted over
it. When the canvas was entered his agent
wired for instructions. He was told, "Wash
off the landscape". He telegraphed back,
"Have washed off the landscape and the old
master. What am I to do with Victor Em-
manuel?" To make a fugitive tale illustrate
a serious truth, whatever different scenes
our canvasses may have acquired in the course
of time there are ineradicable characteristics underneath which we possess in common: ideas, ideals, prejudices—perhaps prejudices above all—and amongst these there is
a sturdy and inflexible determination to do
things in our own way. This common quality
gave rise to your own nationhood, one hundred
and fifty years ago: it is no less the substance
of those nations which make up the British
Empire. There is a certain danger if, in our

enthusiasm, the differences between us are
overlooked. The mutual heritage we enjoy
can create an atmosphere of illusion, because
it is so easy when we have so much in common,
to assume that each of us has a full and complete knowledge of the other. Sir Cecil
Spring-Rice once wrote:

> The fact is, we think that because we speak the
> same language we must think the same thoughts,
> and when one finds that this isn't the case one is
> inclined to be mad.

When we think of a foreign nation, foreign in
a sense that we do not apply to each other, we
assume an ignorance which keeps us from
false assumptions; but in the sphere of Anglo-
American relationships, we may well remember, "a *little* knowledge is a dangerous thing".

We in the British Empire are peculiarly
able to appreciate the philosophy of political
differences, because our own Commonwealth
is based upon them. The modern British Empire is the very consecration of individuality
because within its spacious bounds there is
diversity of religion and language and race,
in fact, every kind of difference which can
divide human beings. And, it seems to me
that, just as the unity of the British Empire
increased and strengthened as the diversity

among its peoples was recognized and accepted, so will the unity of feeling in the English-speaking world grow, as each unit within this congregation of nations learns to understand and respect the other's outlook and needs and difficulties. There is, perhaps, something symbolic of this in our little British family at Washington. His Majesty the King now has four representatives there, each with his own individual responsibility. (A novel and disturbing phenomenon to the old-fashioned student of international law.) But our mutual relations are intimate and cordial and this cordiality, let me say, leads to something even larger—to a sort of co-operative friendship for the great country to which we are severally accredited.

A Canadian's interest in friendship between the British and the American peoples can be taken for granted. Every private individual in Canada is endowed with a natural knowledge of his great neighbour on the one hand, and of his Mother Country, on the other. We know and appreciate the qualities of your greatness, such as the generous idealism, the originality of mind, the power of organization which mark your national life. And we also have a natural knowledge of the country from which we derive so many of our institutions— a knowledge which is born of kinship and tradition. In a degree which increases with the years our affection for the old land grows with a firm confidence in her future which is just as great as our admiration for her past. We Canadians are in the unique position of being able to refer to ourselves as "we North Americans" or as "we British". The wisdom and rightness and profound necessity of an enduring friendship between your people and those of our Empire is an essential article of our political creed.

My purpose to-night, gentlemen, however, is not to talk about subjects on which there are many here who can speak with much deeper knowledge and with far greater power than I. My object is simply to give you my most grateful thanks for the honour you have done me this evening, and to thank you, and through you, the people of the United States, for all that they have done to make my three years here both a memorable experience and an unbroken pleasure. In saying this, I wish to include my wife, because as you know, in the profession of diplomacy, one's wife shares, in full measure, both the happiness and the ardours of the task. I speak, then, for both of us when I say, for all your kindness and your thoughtfulness and for your hospitality, which has been as graceful as it has been sincere, I thank you with all my heart.

A LAND OF PARADOX

Before the Chamber of Commerce of the State of New York, 5th June, 1930

Mr. President and Gentlemen:

I had the pleasure, as your chairman has said, of forgathering with your governing body very shortly after my arrival in this country. On that occasion I first saw this beautiful hall and met the distinguished men who were directing your activities. I shall always remember that visit as one of the most pleasant incidents in the three happy years I have spent in your midst, and I am glad indeed to have a chance to say good-bye to you before I take my leave.

I notice you were founded in 1768, which was only five years after Canada came under the Union Jack, and while this country was under the same flag. We are both, therefore, ancient British contemporaries, you and the Dominion of Canada, and as a representative of the oldest Dominion, I felicitate this ancient British organization (if you will let me call it so), with every good wish for your success and with very sincere congratulations on the distinguished work which you have done over a long period of useful activity.

Your operations extend up to the international border. We know at close hand what you are doing. Your personnel very frequently co-operates with ours on problems of mutual interest. Our business relationships are very closely intertwined, just as are so many other activities in these two countries of ours. In fact, we have a boundary line which, it seems to me, is peculiarly a business frontier. There is a businesslike atmosphere about it which has helped more than we know to maintain that spirit of common sense and neighbourliness which has always prevailed and always will prevail over it. There is, as we know, more business passing over our frontier than over any other civilized border in the world. We have grown to know each other in these two countries to a large extent, because of the interchanges carried on by the business men who move from one side of the border to the other.

Of course you are familiar with Canada by observation, and many of you know our country from end to end. Those of you who know us, know that we have a great many paradoxes and contradictions in our fabric. We are both old and new, new because we have had relatively few years as a unified country, and fewer still as a self-governing nation. We are quite an infant compared to you; but, on the other hand, we are very old, because we have our ancient inherited traditions from Great Britain which we cherish, and we have, too, the legacy of culture from both England and France existing side by side in our Dominion. Again, we are remote from Europe, as you are, working out our destiny side by side with you, with many similarities between us, and yet our historic membership in the British Empire keeps us in touch with the world across the sea, the fortunes of which mean so much to us.

We are larger in area than even your own great Republic, but we are small in population, and the trusteeship of our national treasury rests in the hands of some ten millions of people who are attempting the task of developing our resources and discovering the treasures which we now realize lie beneath our soil. We are a continental nation, and yet we have but one neighbour, with a line fence lying between us which is four thousand miles long.

We have a great influx of foreign capital, most of which comes from you, three and one-

half billions of dollars which you have entrust-
ed to our keeping, and yet we have succeeded
in looking after ourselves to the extent of
owning eighty per cent. of our natural wealth
and holding three-quarters of our national
debt in our own hands. In spite of this, it is
striking to realize that we have been able to
apply to foreign investments, in relation to
our population, greater funds even than you
yourselves have similarly employed.

We are an isolated nation with an ocean on
three sides, to the north, east and west, and
yet we have running across our country one of
the great highways of the world, and shortly
—it is coming without question—we will have
running over us in the sky two or three of
the world's great air routes which may provide a convenient way for you to travel between your great country and the continents
of Asia and Europe.

Again, we are an agricultural country, and
yet we now export more products from our
factories than we do in the form of natural
produce. But I am not here under the courtesy of your hospitality to intrude more on
your time, or to say anything more about our
affairs north of your border. I can only ask
you to come and see for yourselves. If you
do it, I can assure you you will be most wel-

come guests. All I want to do is to say to you,
with all sincerity, and from the heart, how
pleasant you have made my task in these last
three years that I have spent in your midst
as the first Minister which my country sent
to yourselves. This period will always remain for me a most memorable and happy
experience. I cannot tell you how hospitable
and warm-hearted everyone, both in official
and private life, has been, from one end of
your country to the other, and I want to thank
the business community particularly, through
you, for all that they have done—and I have
had the pleasure of meeting many of your
fellow chambers of commerce throughout the
country—to add to this enjoyment. I want
to give you on behalf of Canada, if you will
let me, our sincerest wishes for your success
in the future, and to offer you again our congratulations on your fine record of distinguished service in the past.

THE AMATEUR SPIRIT

Before the University of Michigan at its Annual Commencement, Ann Arbor, 23rd June, 1930

Mr. President and Gentlemen:

A fortnight ago or more, I had the honour to give an address before a distinguished society in New York, in which I formally said good-bye to the people of the United States. And here I am again, in fulfilment of a long-standing invitation, speaking once more on your hospitable soil. I feel that these continued farewells must place me inevitably in the category of those temperamental prima donnas who are induced, for reasons on which I shall not dwell, to say good-bye—not once, but rather too often.

I must say, however, that the fact that my last farewell to an audience in the United States (for such it is) is to be made on academic ground reminds me that some of the happiest hours I have spent since I have been in your midst during the last three and a half years, have been in your universities. I have

343

found time to visit some twenty of these as
I have moved about in my study of the business and governmental activities of your
country, and there are no institutions in your
great Republic which are more typical of the
best in American life, or which are more interesting to the visitor, or which give him a
warmer or more generous welcome. My wife
and I are very happy indeed that we are able,
to-day, to see here in Ann Arbor something
of one of the greatest of those universities of
the United States, which depend directly on
the loyalty and generous support of the state
and which minister so admirably to its needs.

I wondered what I should say to you to-day.
My conscience pricks me when I think that
on such an occasion as this serried ranks of
well-disciplined and well-mannered under-
graduates are exposed as helpless cannon-
fodder to whatever form of visiting artillery
is permitted to open fire on them. I would,
however, much rather regard you as fellow-
gunners than as objects of my fire. I should
like, in fact, to discuss with you, for a few
minutes, some of the forms of shell which
universities use as their educational ammunition.

The shells which are fired are of course
many and varied, for the modern university

can offer the world at large a diversified contribution. For instance, it seems a far cry from the task of supplying practical information direct to farm and municipality to that search in the laboratory or library which has no object but the pursuit of abstract truth. There is a sharp contrast, too, between the professional training of the lawyer, or the business man, or the engineer, and those processes of stimulation and enrichment which we call a liberal education. And yet all of these things are right and necessary, however different they may be.

Is there anything, however, one might ask, which the university can offer all its sons whether they study chemistry or insurance or forestry or Greek, something which all alike may receive and profit by? There are, of course, many gifts with which the university is able to endow all those within its walls, whatever be their course of study. Of these common legacies there is one of which, it seems to me, the modern world might seem to stand peculiarly in need. For lack of a better phrase, shall we call it "The spirit of the amateur"?

It would be prudent without delay to say, not what I mean by the phrase—this will, I hope, appear later—but what I do *not* mean.

The word "amateur" may, of course, conjure
up in our mind a controversy in your country
and mine, as to the ethics and economics of
salaried effort in the world of sport. I have
no intention of touching on this discussion,
however remotely. It is, perhaps, a natural
error to think so literally about a subject as
we do about this. As to the merits of paid
athletes, or unpaid athletes, salaried coaches
or voluntary coaches, we all, no doubt, have
our views, but I do not intend to express mine.
Yet it will not be improper to suggest, that
in this business of the "amateur versus professional", the spirit, as in all else, is surely
more important than the letter.

What, then, should we mean by the "spirit
of the amateur"? It is sometimes useful to
look up derivations and to see the road a
given word has travelled. (Incidentally, I
have a feeling that if no public speaker were
allowed to use any word of three syllables or
more, without defining it, we might find ourselves more reluctant on the public platform
to hurl the epithet of bolshevik, or reactionary,
or chauvinist or cosmopolitan. But this, I
acknowledge, is a digression.) "Amateur",
even the most verdant freshman will know,
means "one who loves", one who pursues an
activity, whatever it may be, *con amore—*

"from the heart". We, of course, know what
it signifies. It is not an external thing, for
at bottom it has nothing to do with money.
We can think of professional pugilists who
have the finest instinct of the sportsman, or
salaried cricketers and baseball players with
a sense of sportsmanship second to none. On
the other hand, although I have never heard of
people paid to play bridge, (to me it would be
a melancholy profession), I have seen grim
faces concentrated with terrifying earnestness
on the outcome of a rubber. Again, we can recall nervous tension on tennis court or golf
course, where recreation and good comradeship should be the rule. And we can remember, too, that an attitude of mind is sometimes
to be found in a college which seems less moved
by the pleasures of the intellectual life than by
a joyless progress toward the degrees and dip-
lomas which are collected like scalps by our
aborigines. This at least we may agree is *not*
the amateur's approach to life.

It may be, of course, that we are becoming
more serious than we used to be, in work and
play as well. Perhaps we are simply becoming more solemn—a very different thing. It
is probably true to say that the last generation has seen a change in our attitude to many
of our activities. A change for the better in

some respects, not, perhaps, in others. There
is now more play. We give more hours to
recreation. The business conscience, for instance, has been sadly shaken by golf. There
is amusing irony in the fact that the most in-
dustrious of countries, Scotland, should have
made such serious inroads on the working
hours of North American business through
this bequest. But we welcome the gift. A
man's productivity is not measured by the
hours he sits behind plate glass. There is
certainly an increasing respect for education
and the value of knowledge. One consequence
of this is that a change of heart has come about
in the world of commerce, which no longer regards a university education as a regrettable
lapse from the serious business of life, to be
lived down with luck, but a definite advantage
in the sphere of practical affairs. This is only
one evidence of the fact that education in all
its forms is constantly gaining in the breadth
of its functions and the importance of its task.

A swiftly increasing belief in knowledge, of
course, may have certain disadvantages. We
are never so characteristically human as when
we confuse the end with the means. If the
very machinery of learning should obscure our
vision we sacrifice our sense of values—which,
may I suggest, is one of the attributes of the

amateur mind. Similarly, sport which misses
its true objective, and is efficient, but devoid
of joy; mechanized recreation which cannot
re-create; knowledge acquired for the sake of
a badge—these are not of the amateur. A
lightness of heart is one of his qualities.

In the last century, it is interesting to observe, the amateur seems to have been thought
to be no blessing. If you dip into the essays
and speeches of a generation ago, both in England and in this country, you will find plenty
of warnings to the youth of the day against
the perils of the amateur spirit, in the sense
in which it was understood. An English
educationist of the time spoke with frankness
of the contemporary youth: "He is no dandy
and no coward, but he is an amateur born
and bred, with an amateur's lack of training,
an amateur's contempt for method and an
amateur's ideal of life." We can sympathize
with this broadside if it is directed against
slackness and inefficiency. It has always, of
course, been characteristic of the young on
both sides of the ocean to sit rather loosely to
knowledge. The undergraduate is habitually
given to an affectation of ignorance and a light-
hearted inconsequence and detachment from
the burdens of learning. There is something
in the Anglo-Saxon character which is slightly

suspicious of erudition. This point of view
has not entirely disappeared from the modern
student. It is, perhaps, related to the ancient
ideal of "muddling through". As in amateur
theatricals we feel somehow, without much
preparation, everything will be "all right on
the night". It is perhaps not unreasonable,
however, to suggest that this attitude is due,
in part, to a healthy reaction from intellectual
priggishness. We can respect a sturdy independence of mind—what might be called a
"selective resistance" to the facts and theories
with which the modern student is confronted.
When I, for two years or so, served as a very
junior don in my old University of Toronto, I
was always uneasy when I saw the students at
my lectures, feverishly taking notes in an ap-
parent effort not to lose any word that fell
from my lips. I was under no flattering de-
lusion as to why they were doing it. Their
effort was to acquire the maximum number of
facts with the minimum amount of effort, and
to return these shop-worn articles as most
unwelcome gifts to the examiner. If I saw
a man sitting still with a thoughtful expression on his face, I knew, of course, that his
mind *might* be on the subject of last night's
dance; but, on the other hand, there was a real
possibility that he was dwelling on the sub-

ject of the lecture, weighing this idea against that, and forming an independent conclusion. In fact, he *might* be thinking.

The amateur in the old sense in which inefficiency was regarded as a virtue is hardly to be found to-day. Our reaction against amateurishness as a cult is seen in the generous extension of public education—the wide application of physical science to industry, the demand for technical training on an unheard of scale—the division and endless subdivision of knowledge into minute branches. With this comes, of course, an accompanying necessity that our sense of proportion should be invoked lest a solemn and indiscriminate respect for data and information should prove an obsession. The educationist of the present day is perhaps less likely to complain of the faults of the amateur than to ask from his students the amateur's spirit of adventure and imagination and sense of proportion. The thoughtful professor nowadays is perhaps less troubled by the amateur point of view than by the over-earnest mind which is weighted with pedantry. One harassed teacher not long ago wrote feelingly of "young men full of refinements and angles, of dreary and distinguished knowledge".

Out of our modern recognition of science

and our dependence upon it has emerged the expert—a new phenomenon essential to society, the product of an age of specialization, an invaluable benefactor in his true relation to the scheme of things as a whole. No branch of knowledge but now requires his services. We depend upon the expert so extensively and have so perfected his education that we seem now to assume, perhaps not unnaturally, that there is a sort of magic in training courses which, given the right formula, can produce *any* given result. There now can be few occupations left which have not courses leading to them—generally under the august auspices of a university. I do not know whether we have yet devised a short intensive course of training for poets or statesmen—probably the first of these is saved from this by the moral of the familiar adage that such products are "born and not made". Not only poets, however, we may well remember, belong to this category.

Someone has said that the expert is an "ordinary man away from home". But that dart, of course, was aimed at the counterfeit article. The real expert is essential to life. Civilization would collapse without trained men with specialized knowledge. Their function, however, is as precise and definite as it is

necessary. Possibly it has not been better
suggested than by the motto of an establishment I once knew where, as it happened,
erudition flowed like water from a spring—
"The expert should be on *tap,* not on *top*".
There is wisdom in this. The expert, whether
his field be electricity or gunnery or law or
forestry or economics or dietetics, may find it
difficult, from his very specialization, to relate his particular subject to the system of
which it is but a part. He has so long studied
the trees that the forest may well be invisible.

It might seem hard to reconcile the attitude
of the specialist with the amateur mind. The
relations between them may well suggest one
of those *"unseen* harmonies" of which the
poets sing. Lord Hewart, the Lord Chief Justice of England, in a recent book, touches on
the issue as it appears in the sphere of government, and tells an agreeable story by way of
illustration. A distinguished Anglo-Indian
civilian, a member of the Indian Civil Service,
returning home on leave after a prolonged
absence, saw the Houses of Parliament on his
way from Victoria to Charing Cross. "What
place is that?" he asked. "That, sir," was the
answer, "is Parliament—the Houses of Parliament." "Really," he exclaimed, though

his exclamation was in fact slightly different, "does that rubbish still go on?"

Here is the issue of the expert versus the amateur. The members of a legislature seem intensely amateurish to the trained administrator, with his workmanlike ideas of getting results. And yet where can one find the amateur spirit in the right sense better shown than in those men who can be found in every parliament—every legislature—who for pure love of the work and a spirit of public service, face the ardours of their task with sportsmanship and a zeal for what they have in hand? We have often heard the man of business commenting on the machinery of government and what he conceives as its untidy methods—what he may call its second-rate product. It is, after all, easy to contrast, on the one hand, a commercial organization which is controlled by a head who can do what he likes, with a legislative body, on the other, in which a compromise betwen conflicting opinions is not only a matter of practice but a matter of duty.

The English-speaking world has been, for the most part, governed by amateurs—such is our tradition. It is true that Gilbert and Sullivan (who reflected the public opinion of their time) satirized the practice in the song

in *H. M. S. Pinafore,* with the immortal refrain.

> Stand close to your desk and never go to sea
> And you all may be Rulers of the Queen's navee!

But the First Lord of the Admiralty is never
an admiral, and the usage followed in the
cabinets of all Anglo-Saxon countries is that
the minister should be an amateur, because,
with that sense of proportion which the amateur point of view transmits, he can relate the
technical problems of his department to the
needs of the public at large. Difficulties come
when the relations are confused. For instance,
legalism is only to be found when the law is
a master and not a servant, just as militarism
comes when the soldier controls the state instead of serving it, and pedantry when learning is not applied to life.

There is, of course, little profit in the controversy between the professional and the
amateur. It is one of those arguments where
there is no right and no wrong, only two rights,
and the answer must embrace them both.
The professional and the amateur soldier have
disagreed since history began, and in a different sphere—the theatre—the same argument
goes on, where actors in both camps balance
the claims of the spontaneity and enthusiasm

and resourcefulness of the amateur against the technical skill and experience and endurance of the professional. But there can be no real quarrel between the expert and the amateur in either field or anywhere in life, because their co-operation is not only reasonable but necessary. A classic example of collaboration is to be found in the relation between judge and jury—the trained and experienced mind on the bench, and the twelve citizens at large whose function is to represent the detachment and uninstructed common sense of the layman. But the harmony between the two points of view can be even more intimate than this. The antithesis between professional and amateur disappears if we use each term in its proper sense, for the two can be blended in the same personality. For instance, the idea of an amateur surgeon, however enthusiastic he might be at his job, would not be a comforting suggestion to the sick, but a trained surgeon with the qualities of the amateur mind, with an amateur's resourcefulness and keenness of brain and passion for his work will, of course, be a better doctor for them, as well as a better man.

The amateur spirit is to be found in both work and play—but possibly leisure is its best criterion. In leisure moments, a man has the

freedom to express himself. He is under no
compulsion, and what he does not only reflects himself, but *is* himself. Perhaps we
have been rather tardy in taking leisure seriously into our educational calculations. Ec-
clesiasticus has observed for our benefit: "The
wisdom of a learned man cometh by opportunity of leisure, and he that hath little business
shall become wise." I am not exactly sure
that this sentiment will find complete favour
with the faculty, nor do I feel that it represents that sort of advice which is likely to be
offered by a well-conducted chamber of commerce. But we know what it means—the noise,
the activity, the movement, the bustle of every-
day life, place the human mind in such a state
of strain as to resist impressions. It is the relaxed and reflective mind that is capable of
receiving the lasting stimulus. Dean Inge has
said: "The soul is dyed the colour of its leisure
thoughts".

It is well, of course, to distinguish between
leisure and idleness. Idleness is an inactive,
negative thing—it represents stagnation. But
leisure suggests that part of our waking life—
perhaps about one-third, in the case of most
people—in which the individual is released
from the mechanism of labour, and leisure
need be no more negative than work itself.

It is, after all, modern life which has produced this sharp distinction between work and play. I suppose that in that ideal state towards which we occasionally cast a somewhat doubtful glance, the gulf between these two will disappear, because every man will have that work which is closest to his heart and there will be no contrast between the chosen task and the labour which is arbitrary. Much of the *malaise* which occurs in industrial life from time to time the world over is due, we know, in a larger proportion than we admit, to the fact that too many human beings are labouring at tasks from which they can derive no pleasure. Not only in the ranks of labour but in all occupations the real self-expression of many must be confined to the hours of freedom. And this, of course, gives even greater importance to the study of that leisure, which happily is now steadily increasing.

What can the university do? I cannot help feeling that the use of leisure is not an unfair test to apply to a liberal education. A college might be contented to be judged partly by the hobbies which its graduates acquire in after years, although I hasten to say that I am not suggesting the creation of a Department of Hobbies in a university, nor even the appointment of a Dean of Hobbies. In an earlier age, such pastimes were of course less common than now. Men who grew up under sterner conditions, a generation or two ago, had too much to do to think much about a hobby. But others acquired, under difficulties, some intelligent activity which eased the strain of their working days and gave them something to think about when these were over. When we hear someone say that he intends "to die in harness", it may mean that, beyond this harness of everyday work, he has no resources to keep him from the boredom of idleness. Thus necessity is made a virtue. A hobby as a matter of normal equipment might prolong many lives in happiness, relieved from business cares, and might too be the indirect cause of such responsibilities being passed to younger shoulders, keen, and perhaps better able, to assume them.

It is, I think, not too much to suggest that the curiosity and keenness and imagination, which are the natural endowment of a liberal education can lead us into an intelligent use of leisure which, to use an overworked word, is not without its *creative* side. A distinguished educationist has said: "Might it not be maintained that leisure was greater than work, because it was the growing time of the spirit, and that life should, therefore, be organized as much, or more, for the sake of leisure as it was for work?" It would be an agreeable task to try to estimate what contribution has been made to the world in leisure hours. (This suggests a subject for a doctorate more useful than many I have seen). One can think at random of the architecture of Jefferson, or the work in physics of Franklin, or of a banker like George Grote who was an historian of Greece as well, or a statesman like Lord Balfour who was a philosopher too. I am reminded of the career of one of our great Canadian railway builders, Sir William Van Horne, for years the head of a great transcontinental system. When one could find, in a first-class mind, such as his, a love of art and a scholar's sense of it (two quite different things), a knowledge of geology and of fungi equally sound, genuine capacity as a painter, the ability to develop a new breed of cattle, real erudition in the lore of Chinese pottery,—all of which were combined with a fine taste for poker—one could see something of the spirit of which amateurs are made.

But the amateur spirit is not confined to a hobby. Nor it it limited to sport or to hours of leisure. It is an attribute of mind which can ennoble everyday work as well as play,

just as imagination can make a living thing
of knowledge. A passion for the game and
a carelessness of victory belong alike to count-
ing-house and law-court and workshop as well
as to the field of sport. Leonardo made of a
dozen crafts a religion of his own. Pasteur
sought the Holy Grail in a laboratory. It is
this spirit that not only can lift sport above
the level of a joyless competition, but can
make an occupation into a vocation, can inform learning with life, and can bring the
knowledge of the expert into the pattern that
gives it meaning.

Robert Bridges in his last great poem, "The
Testament of Beauty", said:

> Hence is the fascination of amateurs in art,
> Who renouncing accomplishment attain the prize
> Of this humbler devotion,— . . .
>
>   . . . .
> Arriving by short-coming, like to homely birds
> Of passage, nesting on the roofs of the workshop.

On the roofs of the workshops as well as
within their walls, in moments of leisure as
in work itself, there is a call for the spirit of
the amateur. One can only suggest its definition. Some one has said that the relay race
is the finest test of sportsmanship, for here
there is no winning, but team-play at its highest; the sacrifice of one to the other to whom

he passes on the "torch". Such sportsmanship as this, together with a consuming enthusiasm, a searching curiosity, and a passion
for achievement—all these has the amateur,
with a sense of quality, a lust for adventure,
a generous mind which is forgetful of the
prize, and above all a zest for life.